Labor Markets
and Unemployment

Wadsworth Series in Labor Economics and Industrial Relations

Lloyd Ulman
Director, Institute of Industrial Relations
University of California, Berkeley

George Strauss
Institute of Industrial Relations
University of California, Berkeley

General Editors

LABOR MARKETS AND UNEMPLOYMENT
Edward Kalachek
Washington University

COMPARATIVE LABOR MOVEMENTS: IDEOLOGICAL ROOTS AND
INSTITUTIONAL DEVELOPMENT
Adolph Sturmthal
University of Illinois

INVESTMENT IN HUMAN CAPITAL
Lester Thurow
Massachusetts Institute of Technology

Labor Markets and Unemployment

Edward D. Kalachek
Washington University

Wadsworth Publishing Company, Inc.
Belmont, California

Editor: Victoria Pasternack

ISBN 0-534-00299-4

L. C. Cat. Card No.: 73-78953

Printed in the United States of America

1 2 3 4 5 6 7 8 9 10—77 76 75 74 73

To keep the price of this book as low as possible, we have used an economical means of typesetting. We welcome your comments.

Series Foreword

Many of today's serious social issues are arising in and are profoundly modifying the labor market and its institutions. These issues include the rights and welfare of ethnic minorities; unionization of white-collar and professional people and strikes in vital public services; inflation, economic growth, and unemployment; automation and job training; antitrust, conglomerates, and coalition bargaining; the injection of heavier doses of union democracy into the collective bargaining process —to name a few. Hence, the labor market provides an excellent "laboratory" for the study of social change.

The analytic techniques now being applied to these problems, however, require new teaching materials. Due weight must be given to these exciting new approaches, for the contemporary undergraduate or graduate student is far less inclined than was his predecessor to sip such new wine out of an old bottle—in this case, the overstuffed and often stultifying textbook. Instructors too (including the undersigned), chafe at the inevitable restraint imposed by the textbook's unitary approach, selection of topics, and order of presentation. Recourse to the library for "supplementary" materials is becoming increasingly difficult and frustrating.

We have tried in this series to alleviate, and we hope eliminate, some of these problems. These books make it easier for the instructor to select specific areas for study and, where necessary, to eliminate others in a particular course. They offer him latitude in arranging the *sequence* of topics according to his own preferences and requirements, as well as a variety of approaches and an opportunity for critical discussion. The viewpoints and approaches of the authors in this series are by no means uniform and homogeneous; nor has any attempt been made to make them so. Neither have we sought to avoid occasional overlapping, which would in any event be unavoidable. What we have attempted to avoid is monotony and the

staleness which can occur when traditional staple fare is up-
dated merely by tacking on additional chapters to deal with
new problems as they emerge.

LLOYD ULMAN
  Professor of Economics
  Director, Institute of Industrial
  Relations
  University of California,
  Berkeley

GEORGE STRAUSS
  Professor of Business
  Administration
  Associate Director, Institute of
  Industrial Relations
  University of California,
  Berkeley

Preface

Labor Markets and Unemployment is designed as core reading
material for courses in labor economics and as a supplementary
text for courses in economic theory and policy. It deals with
the effect of technology and the education explosion on employment and income opportunities. In countless public decisions,
we attempt to reconcile individual employment and income security with economic efficiency and growth. Public policy is
mired in controversy over the severity of the unemployment-
inflation tradeoff. We must try to understand the functioning
of modern labor markets to cope with these issues. This book
seeks to achieve that understanding by synthesizing theory with
empirical research—developing and summarizing some of the more
useful tools in the light of empirical research, and where
fruitful, applying them to public policy.

The author wishes to thank Lloyd Ulman of the University
of California at Berkeley, and Robert Flanagan of the University of Chicago for their insightful comments on the manuscript. Individual chapters have benefited greatly from the
careful reading and criticisms of David Metcalf, Laurence
Meyer, Frederic Raines, and Lawrence Slifman. Chapter 7 and
parts of Chapter 3 were inspired by an earlier collaboration
with Richard R. Nelson and Merton J. Peck. Mrs. Bess Erlich
patiently and tirelessly supervised the typing and preparation
of the final manuscript.

Edward D. Kalachek

Contents

For Sylvia

1

Introduction

This book is concerned with employment and unemployment in today's economy. It deals with the supply and demand for labor, and with the market processes by which jobs and workers are matched. Since the labor market is continuously bombarded by technical change, stress is placed on the contribution to economic growth of a modern, technically trained work force, and on the influence of technical change on that work force.

In the past, most workers were communally employed, or they were serfs, slaves, independent small farmers, or craftsmen. The origins of these work relationships were frequently found in the fortunes of war or in the necessity in a relatively lawless society of trading subservience for security. There is little cause for glorifying traditional work relationships. Their character was neatly captured by Hobbes's description of life as "nasty, brutish, and short." Still poor and ignorant and subject to exploitation though they might be, the mass of workers was relatively secure economically save for catastrophes of war and weather. Demand was highly predictable and reasonably stable. The small farmer produced largely for his own needs. His surplus, if any, was sold mainly in local markets. The craftsman produced largely for surrounding and secure markets, and the serf primarily for his lord. Workers were insured, if poorly so, against the exigencies of age and illness by the kinship system of reciprocal obligation among related members of a culture and by the tradition of noblesse oblige. Likewise, lords, slave owners, farmers, and master craftsmen were relatively secure in the possession of a home-grown and home-trained labor supply. The masters were likely to reap the rewards of raising and training a work force, due to the many impediments to mobility. This security was brought to an end by the gradual growth of markets and the subsequent specialization of labor and improvements in production techniques. The Industrial Revolution inaugurated a still continuing era of rapid economic growth and rising living standards.

1

As an aftermath of the Industrial Revolution, production was
increasingly characterized by larger scale enterprises, by the
utilization of large quantities of capital, and by the specialization of labor. Recognizing the efficiency of a central
energy source (the steam engine) and the expensive machinery it
required resulted in the factory. The predominance of the factory led to the predominance of wage and salary employment.
 Work is the central activity of human existence in the
modern industrial society. It is economically and socially important for all except the most and the least fortunate. The
choice of occupation and degree of success effectively molds a
person's life style. Work relationships determine not only the
amount of market goods and services at one's command, but they
also determine status, the nature of social options, and one's
potential sense of achievement. If we know a man's occupation
—whether he is an engineer, an accountant, a semiskilled steel
worker, or a bus driver—we know much about him. The growth in
income and in the size of markets, the specialization of labor,
and the institutional form of the labor market evolved in Western society in the past two centuries have subjected the per-
manence and attractiveness of the central human activity of
work to determination by the impersonal forces of supply and
demand. Traditionally, workers have abhorred wage and salary
employment. Indeed, the strong prejudice in favor of self-
employment, the desire to be one's own boss and to work at
one's own pace clearly persists today. Nonetheless, most workers labor for wages and salaries. Seven million persons, or
only nine percent of the work force were self-employed in 1970.
As recently as 1948, the figure was around 11 million persons,
20 percent of a smaller labor force.
 Labor services are sold in markets not too dissimilar to
the markets for cars and used houses. Wage and salary employment represents a contractual rather than a status relationship.
Things are changing rapidly now, but most workers do not yet
possess very strong property rights in their jobs. Their employers have no socially required or legally sanctioned obligation to assure a minimum of sustenance and welfare over any
protracted period of time. Employees are exposed to the insecurity of short work weeks, layoff or discharge in the event of
recession, secularly declining demand, technical change, or inadequate personal performance. In addition to being insecure,
wage and salary relationships, except for the most casual and
low paying jobs, require a considerable amount of self-discipline and an ability to accommodate one's personality to the
requirements of the production process. The normal employee
works at a speed, at a place, at a time, and under conditions
stipulated by others. He can be disciplined or discharged for
insubordination or incompetence. He undertakes a personality
subordination completely unsanctioned by anything except the

market place and by the belief that his position in the work
hierarchy reflects merit.

Reliance on the market place is twofold: the employer is
as dependent as the worker; the employer depends on the market
for workers. Consequently, the employer is always subject to
the risk that workers will go elsewhere in search of better
wages or better working conditions, or simply for new experiences. The proper performance of a job of any complexity requires appropriate work attitudes, a certain amount of background knowledge and experience, and a familiarity with the
specific production process. These attributes are not cost-
lessly embodied in workers. Education and training require
resources. At the same time, most training raises potential
productivity in a variety of activities. It increases the
worker's mobility and the wage level to which he can aspire
realistically. If the employer pays for the training, he must
frequently give the worker at least some of its fruits in the
form of higher wages, or else the trainee may take his newly
acquired skill to another employer. The difficulties of capturing the benefits of training inhibits employer investment
and keeps it below the socially optimum level. To an appreciable extent, the quality of the work force will be determined
by training that occurs away from the work situation. The educational system and the value structure of the society play a
vital role in determining worker attitudes and competence.

This is no small matter. Until recently, it was popularly
believed that the economic growth process was dominated by the
acquisition of physical capital. Per capita economic growth
was explained by increases in the amount of capital per worker.
That is, we had higher income than our ancestors because we
produced more per hour than they did. We produced more because
we could afford to provide workers with bulldozers rather than
shovels, and with computers rather than desk calculators. Belief in the catalytic role of capital was first shaken by the
rapid recovery of the skilled and industrious populations of
Germany and Japan from the wartime devastation of their capital
stocks. Next, we witnessed the limited ability to absorb capital of the poorly educated populations of Asia, Africa, and
Latin America. Finally, work done at the National Bureau of
Economic Research by John Kendrick, Solomon Fabricant, and
others indicated that about half of the economic growth of the
United States during the twentieth century could be explained
by increases in capital and labor inputs. Between 1889 and
1957, labor input grew at an annual rate of 1.4 percent, and
physical capital input at an annual rate of 2.5 percent. A
weighted combination of labor and capital inputs grew at an
annual rate of 1.7 percent. Physical output grew twice as
fast, at an annual rate of 3.5 percent. In the period between
1919 and 1957, output actually grew three times as fast as

input.[1] There is reason to believe that this discrepancy between output and input growth would be substantially smaller if improvements in the health and education of the work force and technical advance were taken into account. Further, technical advance itself is strongly influenced by the quality of the work force. Today, most innovations are electronic or chemical. They are based on research efforts by scientists and engineers. They require trained and highly flexible managers, salesmen and production work forces for their implementation and dissemination. Knowledge in the minds of men appears to be one of the catalytic factors underlying economic growth.

The positive value of economic growth is too obvious to merit much discussion. Let those in doubt compare the work conditions and living standards of today with those of the last century, or let them observe how people live in such areas as Macedonia, which have been relatively untouched by modern economic progress. Still, the economic implementation of the technical knowledge of some workers does result in hardship, unemployment, and adjustment problems for other workers. The growth process is uneven. Changes in productivity are not evenly distributed throughout the economy. They bunch in a limited number of activities. The rise in real income, which they spur, is not necessarily spent in the technically progressive industries nor is it evenly spread throughout the economy. Rather, the demand for such luxury products as boats and stereo equipment rises sharply. Demand for such staples as food may be little changed, and demand for some inexpensive and inferior products may actually decline. Growth thus involves the expansion of some firms and industries and the demise of others. It involves new and superior products and processes superseding established ways of doing things. New skills are developed; old ones become obsolete. Technical change and economic growth necessarily involve changes in the importance of different occupations and in the geographic and industrial locations of jobs. Some jobs are eliminated. Some workers are thrust into unemployment. New jobs are likely to be created, but they may be in different firms or geographic areas. The skills and educational backgrounds required for the new jobs may not be possessed by the displaced workers.

The fear that workers and jobs may not easily match is common. Legislators, union leaders, and many informed citizens fear that the ingenuity, creativity, and drive of the highly educated and skilled members of the labor force may be condemning their less well-endowed brethren to permanent joblessness.

---

[1] Solomon Fabricant, *Basic Facts on Productivity Change*, Occasional Paper 63 (New York: National Bureau of Economic Research, Inc., 1959), p. 19.

In recent decades, technical change and capital accumulation have reduced the number of jobs requiring mainly physical strength and endurance, particularly in agriculture, but also in manufacturing, construction, and the household. This skill bias resulting from technical change is leading to the elimination of physical drudgery—surely a desirable outcome. Is it also leading to a dearth of opportunity for those whose genetic endowment or training has qualified them only for unskilled or semiskilled jobs?

In the course of history, a regime of security for the individual as a worker but of stagnation for the individual as a consumer has been replaced by a regime of consumer progress purchased at the cost of worker insecurity. Much of the social and manpower legislation of the past four decades represents an effort to redress this imbalance. The reconciliation of individual security and economic progress remains, however, a key problem as the government becomes increasingly involved in organizing the labor market and in protecting the individual against economic calamity. This book is concerned with these problems. It seeks to describe some of the contributions made by human labor to economic progress and the influence of economic activity and development on the utilization of labor and on the security of its sellers.

In Chapter 2 we discuss the quantity of labor, and in Chapter 3 the quality. Increasingly, changes in quality have been the vital factor in augmenting input and output. Quality still remains an elusive concept. Our knowledge of its production and characteristics is mainly intuitive and implicit. Chapter 4 deals with the search procedures that result in matching heterogeneous workers and jobs. It concentrates on the processes that lead to a reconciliation between the requirements of employers and the aspirations of workers. Chapter 5 is a fresh treatment of the anatomy, functions, causes, and cures of unemployment. Chapter 6 analyzes the incidence of unemployment and presents the hotly debated unemployment-inflation dilemma. Since the continuing process of technical change effectively structures modern labor markets, any adequate analysis of employment and unemployment must also treat the problems of an advancing technology. This relationship is developed throughout the book and summarized in Chapter 7.

2

Labor Supply and the Labor Force

What do we mean by the *aggregate supply of labor*? It is not an easy question to answer. We must decide first what we mean by *labor* and second what we mean by *supply*. In the broadest sense, labor has both quantity and quality dimensions. The term refers to the talents, the capabilities, and the capacity for producing goods and services that people bring to their work. More narrowly, labor is simply the amount of time people are willing to put forth in work situations. The broad view recognizes sharp interpersonal differences in the quality of time and effort, and deals with efficiency units. Two different individuals placed on the same job and given the same co-operating factors will produce quite different amounts of output. An average American worker is capable of producing more in an hour than an average Chinese worker. Isaac Stern creates more pleasure for his listening audience in any given performance than does the average violinist. An hour of effort by an electrical engineer represents more labor input—will contribute more to final output—than will an hour of effort by an unskilled worker. The narrower view aggregates individuals and treats one hour of input as the equivalent of another. A rose is a rose is a rose. An hour supplied by the corner newsboy receives the same value as an hour supplied by a crack tool and die maker.

The supply concept that weights people by their productive capacity—that treats an unskilled worker as one unit of input and a skilled worker as some multiple of one—is certainly the more interesting concept. After all, quality improvement has been the most important labor supply development of recent decades. It probably represents the major explanation of recent per capita economic growth. In contrast, changes in the quantity of labor account for only a modest fraction of the rise in aggregate output, and for none of the recent rise in per capita output. Unfortunately, quality defies satisfactory measurement and can be treated only in an impressionistic fashion, whereas

6

labor quantity is quite susceptible to measurement. Still, quantity must have its due. At times, it is useful to treat individuals as though they were homogeneous units of labor. If we wish to know how many jobs are necessary to create full employment, it is practical to weight workers equally and add one to the next. If we wish to know how rapidly average productivity or economic well-being is increasing, we must divide output or income by the total number of workers. We shall discuss quantity in this chapter and quality in the next.

In the popular mind, labor supply is simply the number of manhours people are working or seeking to work at any moment of time. Its facets can be summed as follows: manhours available = population × proportion of the population available for work × number of hours annually available for work. Except for societies in which immigration is quantitatively important, the existing population of working age effectively establishes the outer bound of the labor supply. Since population size reflects earlier demographic trends, the outer bound is determined by events and decisions of the near, far, and very far past. The age composition as well as the size of the population are important since physical and legal limitations inhibit work effort by the very young and the very old. Children contribute little market effort until they are 16 or 17 years of age. Consequently, the outer limits of the labor supply are not very responsive to short-run economic pressures. The actual labor supply falls short of the outer limits, of course. The population devotes considerably less time and effort to work than what would be physiologically possible. Labor supply thus depends on work motivation. To take an extreme example, supply should be considerably greater during wartime, when patriotism, social pressure, and duress are stimulating effort, than during peacetime. Indeed, the labor supply may then approximate the outer physiological bounds.

If the strength of the factors motivating supply changes over time, we will provide only limited information if we follow popular practice and define supply as the amount actually forthcoming in any given time period or as the maximum feasible amount forthcoming. Rather, the most useful approach is to define a *supply schedule*—a functional relationship between the willingness to work and the value of motivational forces. Economic incentives—wages—may represent the most important of these motivational forces. An analogy might be helpful here. Suppose we are interested in explaining or predicting behavior in the copper market. It would then be useful to know how much copper was actually supplied last year and for some purposes it might be useful to know proven world reserves of copper ore. What would be most useful, though, is some knowledge of what causes the supply of copper to vary from year to year. We are immediately confronted with the facts that some ore bodies are cheaper to mine than others, and that copper companies appear to be motivated in their production decisions by the urge toward maximum profits. Hence, we can postulate that the supply of copper is a function of its market price; as price rises, copper companies will mine increasingly higher cost ore bodies. As price declines, they will restrict their effort to the lower cost bodies. Using modern statistical techniques to estimate the slope of the copper supply curve, we can then determine how much additional supply will be induced by a rise in price. The definition of supply as a functional relationship provides powerful insight into the operation of copper markets. So long as we are correct in our postulate and successful in our efforts at statistical estimation, we will be able to predict how output and price will respond to changes in the demand for copper.

Returning to the labor market, and seeking equivalent explanatory power, we must move beyond knowledge of the fact that a monthly average of 84 million Americans was either working or looking for work in 1971; and that those who were working averaged 39.3 hours of work per week. We must seek to discover how willingness to work varies depending on economic incentives. Since total labor supply is simply the aggregation of individual labor supplies, we shall begin by explaining the behavior of the individual decision making unit.

THE THEORY OF LABOR SUPPLY

When we hunt for the economic element underlying an individual's work decision, we are looking for something far more subtle than the rule that one must work to eat.[1] A very appreciable portion of the population could satisfy its physiological needs and meet minimum standards of decency while working far fewer hours than are currently customary. Economic motivation is not a matter of brute survival but a question of how many consumer goods and how much financial security to purchase. For most people, the work decision is not a simple "yes" or "no" matter. It is rather a question of how much work and how much leisure one desires. How many weeks of work per year and how many hours per week? The factory worker must choose between activities in which overtime is likely and activities in which it is unusual. Along with many other workers, he must decide

---

[1]This treatment parallels the presentation in Edward D. Kalachek and Fredric Q. Raines, "The Labor Supply of Low Income Workers," in *Technical Studies, The President's Commission on Income Maintenance Programs* (Washington, D.C.: U.S. Government Printing Office, 1970), pp. 159-181.

whether or not to moonlight. The school teacher must decide
whether to work after school and during the summer and semester
intervals. The housewife must decide whether to work in the
market full- or part-time, and if part-time, how many days per
week.

We assume that people are motivated to make work decisions
by a desire to maximize their satisfaction or utility. They
are guided by the urge to choose more, and to avoid less, satisfactory forms of behavior. Leisure is a source of satisfaction, and the more the better. On the other hand, work results
in income, which can be used to purchase goods and services, a
source for most of considerable satisfaction. Leisure and consumption goods (the outcome of work) are thus both desired.
Hard choices must be made, given that most people receive their
income primarily from work, and that there are only 24 hours to
the day. Each decision unit must select the combination of
leisure and income that maximizes its satisfaction. It must
weigh the benefits of leisure against the benefits of additional goods and services.

The wage rate plays a crucial role in choosing between
leisure and income. It represents the amount of goods and
services that can be obtained as a reward for desisting from an
hour of leisure. It is the bribe for relinquishing time that
could be devoted to sleep, reading, lying on the beach, or playing with one's children. What impact will changes in the wage
rate have on the willingness to supply labor and to forego leisure? The relationship between the wage rate and the willingness to work is surprisingly complex. Changes in the wage rate
have both income and substitution effects. At any level of effort, with higher wages, income will be higher. At higher income levels, people wish to purchase more of all normal goods.
This certainly includes leisure. The relationship between income and desired work input will thus be negative. At higher
incomes, people will purchase more leisure. Since there are
only 24 hours to the day, they will do less work. But that is
only half the story. Higher wages mean that leisure has become
more expensive relative to goods and services. The demand
schedules for normal goods slope downward. When the price of
cantaloupe rises relative to the price of honeydew melon, we
substitute against cantaloupe in our consumption budgets,
purchasing fewer cantaloupes. Likewise, when the price of leisure rises, we substitute against it, and use more of our en-
ergies to purchase goods and services that are now relatively
cheaper. The substitution effect on work will thus be positive.
Operating through the substitution effect, higher wages induce
longer hours of work.

Suppose a maiden aunt were to die, leaving you a $1,000
annuity. In this instance, there would be no need to disen-
tangle income and substitution effects. The price of leisure

would be unaffected. You would simply have more income and
would move to a higher level of satisfaction, purchasing more
goods and services and more leisure. Consider another example.
Your wage rate is increased, both raising the price of leisure
and moving you to a higher level of potential income and satisfaction. Now we conduct a small experiment. We lower your
level of nonwork related income—annuities, dividends, interest
—until you are restored to the satisfaction level existing
prior to the wage increase. There is no longer an income effect, only a relative price change. We can thus observe the
operation of the price substitution effect. Leisure is more
expensive, and so you will buy less leisure and work longer
hours.

These examples should help to clarify the principles involved. In the real world, though, pure income and pure substitution effects are somewhat difficult to observe. Most frequently we confront a wage change that naturally embodies both
an income and a substitution effect. The income and substitution effects have directly opposite impacts on the willingness
to work. Which will predominate? Will high wages induce more
or less work? Will the supply schedule of labor (defined as a
function of the real wage) be positively or negatively sloped?
If the substitution effect dominates, the supply schedule will
be positively sloped. People will work more when offered higher wages. On the other hand, if the income effect dominates,
the supply schedule will bend backward. People will work less
when offered higher wages. The outcome of the struggle depends
on tastes. There is no a priori reason why either effect
should always predominate. A worker who attains, in Boulding's
phrase, "the income of his heart's desire," will certainly reduce his work effort in response to higher wages. However, an
aspiration income level need not be invoked to justify a backward bending supply schedule. All that is required is the dominance of the income effect.

Leisure and work are so defined that they exhaust the
day's 24 hours. Since leisure is defined as a source of satisfaction, work as the alternative usage of time is implicitly
treated as a source of relative disutility. The reader will
recognize this as a cursory treatment of an important topic.
Formal economic theory abstracts from a host of intriguing
questions regarding the relationship between work and human
satisfaction. Clearly, individual attitudes toward work are
highly varied depending on the nature of the individual personality and the nature of the production process. Casual observation and opinion surveys both suggest that physical fatigue,
danger, emotional pressures, or constraints on freedom of movement make work a bore or a displeasure for many. For others,
work is fun independent of the compensation received. The
work place does provide an outlet for urges toward status,

creativity, and social contact. Freud stressed the importance of work in binding the individual more closely to reality. It is a commonplace that retirement can lead to psychological and physical deterioration. Popular recognition of the intrinsic necessity of work for some is reflected in the adage: "The devil finds work for idle hands."

We must leave the treatment of these topics to the industrial psychologist and sociologist, summarizing for our purposes in the following fashion. Since individual tastes vary, so will the positions and slopes of individual supply curves. People who detest work will labor less than others and will respond to higher wages with unusually avid purchases of leisure. People who, at the appropriate margin, receive more satisfaction from work than from leisure will toil at close to the physiologically maximum rate, regardless of compensation. Many of us can attest to the existence of such work oriented people, but an impressive array of evidence, to be presented later, suggests that they are a minority. If market work is a source of positive satisfaction, something people would engage in at a zero hourly wage, that satisfaction erodes for most long before the standard work week is attained.

The functional relationship between market work and wages represents only the first facet of the theory of labor supply. Further useful elaborations are possible. First, we should recognize that work can occur either within or without the market place. Keeping house, raising children, and attending school are important instances of nonmarket work. Indeed, it is "a close approximation to the truth to regard the average American household as a small factory, highly equipped with labor saving devices."[2] The wage rate for market effort is explicit and normally paid in the form of generalized purchasing power. A certain number of dollars and cents are received, which can be used to purchase any of the goods and services sold in the market place. In contrast, the wage rate for home effort is normally implicit and particularized. Home pay normally consists of the goods and services one has produced at home. Since the market and home wage rates generally differ except in equilibrium positions, and since market activities are of particular interest, market and nonmarket work will be analyzed separately.

Once we allow for nonmarket activities, the market wage rate becomes the price of leisure and of home-produced goods, relative to market goods. Higher wage rates permit substitution against both homework and leisure. The additional leisure that higher income purchases can come either from less market

---

[2]A. K. Cairncross, "Economic Schizophrenia," *Scottish Journal of Political Economy*, February 1958.

work or from less homework. Substitution against homework is
possible since many goods produced in the household can also be
purchased in the market place. Even if their total labor supply schedule is backward bending, men earning high wages may
choose to work as many market hours as those receiving lower
compensation. If their market productivity is substantially
higher than their home productivity, they will rationally take
additional leisure by hiring others to do such things as gar-
dening, lawn mowing, house painting, and car washing. Similarly, women with high market productivity may achieve additional
leisure by hiring maids, buying convenience foods, shopping at
groceries that accept orders over the telephone and deliver,
and having beauticians come to their houses rather than going
to beauty parlors.

The worker can now be regarded as having a utility function whose arguments are consumption goods purchased either in
the market place or produced at home and leisure. He seeks to
maximize utility, given market wage rates, home productivity,
potential nonwage and salary income, and a number of other factors. The amount of labor supplied to the market will depend,
for instance, on financial obligations, such as the presence of
debt or of dependents to be fed, housed, and clothed. Dependents have a two-edged effect: they increase income requirements
and stimulate market effort on the part of the husband. On the
other hand, if the dependents are either very young or very old
or ill, they will require care and supervision, thus raising
the nonmarket productivity of the wife and discouraging her
market participation.

Who makes these labor supply decisions? A single person
living alone and self-supporting normally constitutes an auton-
omous decision making unit. But most Americans live in family
units in which some pooling of income and some sharing of home
tasks occurs. In a family, decision making on labor supply involves joint consultation. Such communal aspects mean that the
participation of each family member is dependent not only on
his own wage but also on that of every other family member, and
on the potential family income.[3] Complex relationships between
one's own wage rate and labor supply can then eventuate. For
instance, a higher wage rate for the family head can lead to

---

[3]The assumption that the family behaves as though it had a
joint utility function has never been adequately elaborated or
tested. Empirically, it is clear that the economic potential
of husbands affects the work decisions of wives, and the potential of parents the decisions of children, but the reciprocity
of these relationships is open to question. Family decision
making may better be described by a recursive rather than a
fully simultaneous model.

more market work, but also leads to the performance of fewer
home tasks for him, and to more home and less market work for
his spouse. There is strong evidence that the wives of high
wage husbands do less market work than the wives of low wage
husbands. In low wage families, both husband and wife are
likely to be working and presumably to be sharing home chores.
In high wage families in which the husband is the high wage
earner, he is likely to take his leisure by avoiding home tasks.
His wife is likely to take her leisure by avoiding market tasks.
    The family's labor supply decision will profoundly affect
its living style. It will determine the degree of economic security to which the family can aspire, the amount of consumption goods at its disposal, and the leisure available for its
enjoyment. Wage rates change frequently but labor supply decisions are so basic that they are adjusted only lethargically.
Economists are inclined to believe, with some supporting evidence, that the family's labor supply decision is based on its
expectations of income from labor and other sources over the
intermediate term horizon rather than on the basis of actual
current earnings. The hierarchial nature of much of American
industry encourages workers to gauge their labor supply to potential income. Most manufacturing firms, for instance, require the same number of manhours per year from their production employees regardless of rank or earnings. The low level
semiskilled worker normally labors as long as the senior level
semiskilled worker, though he may earn substantially less per
hour. Experience and seniority are the prerequisites for advancement in wages. They can be obtained only by working with
reasonable competence for the required number of manhours per
year. The labor supply response of the semiskilled worker who
fulfills the company's manhour expectations cannot be attributed to his current wage, but rather to the average discounted
wage expected during his stay with the company. Likewise, the
assistant professor undoubtedly labors at least as long and
hard as the full professor though for considerably less compensation. His efforts are motivated not so much by his current
earnings as by his expectations of advancement.

THE LABOR FORCE

    Unfortunately, aggregate economic quantities cannot be
perceived directly. The economic universe is too large and too
complex to permit accurate personal observations on the state
of employment, unemployment, or the labor supply. Rather, it
is necessary to define what is meant by such concepts and then
to devise measuring techniques and data collection systems. We
are cast inevitably into a world of imprecision and incomplete-
ness. To begin with, there is no single definition of any

important social science concept that will prove uniquely superior for all purposes. The preferred definition depends on
the use to be made of the data. Only one series is likely to
be collected, and it is likely to be put to many uses. Consequently, the operational definition selected is likely to be a
compromise, ideal for no purpose. A second compromise must be
arranged between conceptual purity and the high cost of collecting data. Consequently, statistical series inevitably provide
imperfect, and hence distorting, measures of the phenomena they
seek to describe.

Forewarned, let us turn to the data collection system and
set of definitions used in measuring key labor market phenomena.
Once a month, a set of well-trained enumerators, mainly middle
class housewives working part-time, interview a stratified random sample of about 47,000 households. The survey is conducted
by the U.S. Bureau of the Census and its results are published
by the U.S. Department of Labor, Bureau of Labor Statistics in
Employment and Earnings. The responses of the households interviewed are weighted according to the geographic and demographic characteristics of respondents, and are then generalized into totals representative of the entire U.S. population.
Forty-seven thousand households comprise an enormous sample,
resulting in a minimal sampling error for the major labor force
magnitudes. For instance, 95 out of 100 times, the monthly labor force estimate deviates from the true labor force by less
than 380,000 persons, and the monthly unemployment estimate deviates from the true estimate by less than 150,000 persons.
These are small deviations, given that the labor force averaged
84 million persons and unemployment 5 million persons in 1971.

Normally, when the enumerator calls, the housewife is the
only person at home. She will be interviewed for herself and
for all other household members aged 16 and over. If other
members of the household are present, they will answer for
themselves. Each respondent is asked: "What were you doing
most of last week?" If the respondent does not reply that he
or she was working (or physically unable to work), the next
question will be: "Did you do any work at all last week, not
counting work around the house?" A "no" answer will elicit yet
another probe: "Did you have a job (or business) from which you
were temporarily absent last week?" All those who did any work
at all for pay or profit, or did as much as 15 hours of nonpaid
labor in a family owned enterprise are classified as employed.
Persons who did not work during the survey week but had jobs
from which they were temporarily absent because of illness, vacation, bad weather, strikes, or personal reasons are also classified as employed. Employment dominates unemployment in the
definitional system. A person with a job during part of the
week is classified as employed even if he lost or left the job
at some time during the week. A person with a job who is hunt-

ing for another job is also classified as employed. Employment
also dominates unemployment in the interviewing process. If
and only if the first three questions do not indicate some current employment status is the respondent asked: "Have you been
looking for work during the past four weeks?"
      All those without a job during the survey week, who made
specific efforts to find a job during the preceding four weeks,
and who were available for work during the survey week (or
would have been available except for temporary illness), are
classified as unemployed. Persons without jobs but waiting to
report within 30 days to a new wage and salary job, and persons
on layoff waiting for recall are also classified as unemployed.
As so defined, unemployment is quite a different thing than
eligibility for unemployment compensation, and properly so.
The person without prior work experience, the person whose
prior work experience was in an uninsured job, the person with
brief job tenure, the person who exhausted benefits or was
otherwise disqualified is not eligible for unemployment compensation. Nonetheless, if he lacks a job and is looking for
work, he is unemployed. The government publishes a separate
series on insured unemployment, drawn directly from the unemployment compensation records. In 1970, unemployment averaged
4.1 million persons per month, whereas only 1.8 million persons
drew unemployment compensation.
      From the employment and unemployment statistics and popu-
lation totals collected monthly, a number of useful auxiliary
concepts can be derived. The civilian labor force is derived
simply by adding employment and unemployment. The civilian labor force participation rate is derived by dividing the civilian labor force by the civilian noninstitutional population of
working age. The unemployment rate is derived by dividing unemployment by the civilian labor force. Note that respondents
are not directly asked about their labor force status. Labor
force is a derivative concept. It is simply the sum of the employed and the unemployed. Data is collected on the demographic characteristics and recent industrial and occupational
affiliations of respondents. Consequently, we are not restricted to summary statistics for the entire population.
Rather, labor force, employment, and unemployment statistics
are available for a wide range of age, sex, race, marital status, occupational, and industrial groups.

The Relationship between Labor Supply and the Labor Force

      Even noted economists make the error of confusing labor
force with labor supply. Useful as the labor force measure is,
we should avoid this confusion. Labor supply is a schedule indicating manhour availability as a function of real wages,

given tastes, needs, and income from nonwork related sources. The labor force is something quite different. Participation in the labor force represents only one dimension of work effort. It is simply one facet of a measure of manhour availability. This more interesting measure can be obtained as the cross-product of weeks worked or looking for work, of hours worked or looking for work per week, and of labor force participation. The raw material for its construction is available since the Census Bureau also collects data on weeks worked and average hours worked. However, an estimate of total manhours will not yield a point on an authentic labor supply function. The labor force series is too limited and too simple for this purpose. It captures only some of the persons involved in work. The woman performing housework for her own family is excluded. If maids, governesses, waitresses, and chefs did the same work, they would all be enumerated as labor force members. The full-time student is excluded. A factory worker producing capital goods (an activity analogous to the full-time student's) is included. The hours of the hobbyist making furniture for his family in his basement workshop are not counted, although the hours of a worker in a furniture factory are enumerated.

Labor force membership involves a market test. Persons engaged in productive efforts outside the market place are not counted. The exclusion is partially a matter of practicality. Hours of nonmarket work cannot be readily or accurately estimated. A highly reasonable policy bias is also involved. One major purpose of the labor force series is to provide information on the number of market jobs that must be generated to maintain full employment. Since social concern and public policy focus on market jobs, that is what the series measures. If the proportion of housewives, students, and hobbyists were to remain constant over time, their exclusion would result in an understatement of the number of persons engaged in productive activity, but would still leave a clear view of trends. The proportion of effort devoted to nonmarket activities, however, has been anything but constant. Consequently, we shall have to be alert in analyzing labor force trends to make sure we do not interpret shifts between nonmarket and market activity as shifts in labor supply.

Its narrow scope of coverage aside, the labor force series measures current activity as perceived by the respondent rather than availability under stipulated circumstances. Due to two major conceptual deficiencies, the labor force data do not necessarily provide even a point on a supply schedule of market labor. First, since unemployment and eligibility for unemployment compensation are quite different matters, the labor force may include some unemployed persons who are willing to work, but who will not work at the going real wage for their services. These persons provide an authentic part of the market labor

supply only at significantly higher wages than those currently
prevailing. Second, the number of persons in the labor force
may be affected by the current level of demand for labor. If
so, under less than full employment circumstances, the labor
force will not be an accurate indicator of the number of workers available at full employment. The theory of labor supply
bases family work decisions on wage rates and property income
(dividends, interest, rent, and other income received from nonwork related sources) expected for individual family members
over their planning horizon. These expectations can be temporarily jarred by illness or by sudden declines in demand. The
involuntary joblessness of a family member will require some
adjustments in economic planning. The family must either draw
from available savings, reduce current consumption standards,
or temporarily increase the labor input of other members. All
available evidence indicates that the family normally wishes to
maintain its living standards.

A likely hypothesis is that the involuntary income loss of
one family member will encourage increased market input by
other family members. The unexpected unemployment of the husband may turn the wife into a job hunter. This is known as the
additional worker hypothesis, and was first proposed during the
1930s by W. S. Woytinsky. The additional worker hypothesis was
stimulated by a postcard survey that showed an extremely high
level of unemployment. Woytinsky argued that the unemployment
level overstated the number of jobs needed if we were to reach
full employment. Find a job for the husband, and unemployment
will be reduced by two, since the wife will drop out of the labor force. The additional worker hypothesis soon generated an
adversary in the *discouraged worker hypothesis*. From the perspective of a potential worker, the effective wage rate associated with any job may be calculated as the wage rate times the
probability per unit of time of securing the job. When unemployment is high, its average duration is also high. This
leads to high real and psychic search costs for those seeking
work. A job paying $2 an hour is only worth $1 an hour for the
first year if six months of search is required to secure the
job. High unemployment thus causes some to postpone labor
force activity until a subsequent, more felicitous time. Discouraged workers are willing to work at going wage rates but
are not hunting for jobs, due to the currently adverse probability of finding them.

During the Great Depression of the 1930s, the additional
and discouraged worker effects were presented as competing hypotheses. Now it is clear that they are not mutually exclusive
alternatives. Rather, they describe different types of behavior that can and do occur simultaneously. When unemployment
is high, finding a job will involve an unusually discouraging,
time-consuming, and expensive effort. Some will be discouraged,

shrinking the size of the labor force. On the other hand, when unemployment is high, the dependents of unemployed workers will be tempted to hunt for jobs to buttress family finances. This will swell the size of the labor force. What is the net result of these two gross effects? Does the size of the labor force at less than full employment understate or overstate its size at full employment? This answer is important for estimating the losses in output associated with high unemployment and for determining the number of jobs necessary for restoring full employment. For instance, assume that the labor force is composed of 80 million persons, and that the unemployment rate is seven percent. For present purposes, tentatively accept four percent unemployment as full employment. (The concept of full employment will be fully explored in Chapter 5.) If additional and discouraged worker effects are of equal magnitude, then 2.4 million additional jobs are required to attain full employment. On the other hand, if the discouraged worker effect dominates, excess unemployment will exceed 2.4 million persons. Some of the unemployment will be hidden. More than 2.4 million additional jobs will be required to restore full employment. Workers will be encouraged to enter the labor market as employment expands. The labor force will be larger at four percent than it was at seven percent unemployment.

The evidence strongly suggests that during moderate recessions, the discouraged worker effect exceeds the additional worker effect. The actual labor force thus understates the size of the labor force at full employment. Estimates of the magnitudes involved vary considerably. While hidden unemployment was once regarded as being of major magnitude, the best current estimate appears to be that a 1.0 percentage point rise in the unemployment rate will reduce the labor force participation rate by about 0.2 percentage point.[4]

The unemployment rate thus understates the amount of output loss and the amount of human suffering associated with recession or the onset of economic slack. The significance of these additional losses is questioned by Jacob Mincer. Very few adult men of prime working age are discouraged by high unemployment from active labor force participation. The ranks of the discouraged consist primarily of housewives, and also noticeable numbers of teenagers and older men. Mincer argues that lifetime labor force participation depends on longer-run variables such as property income, permanent wage rates, and permanent home productivity. Most housewives will spend only a

---

[4]See Jacob Mincer, "Labor Force Participation and Unemployment: A Review of Recent Evidence" in *Prosperity and Unemployment*, eds., Robert A. and Margaret S. Gordon (New York: John Wiley and Sons, Inc., 1966), pp. 73-112.

portion of their adult lives in the labor force. The timing of
such participation will rationally depend on current or transitory values of the income, wage rate, and home productivity
variables. A rational woman would enter the labor force during
those years when her market productivity was highest relative
to her home productivity. She would be least likely to work
when her children were young, and more likely when they were
grown. For the same reason, cyclical variations in wage rates
or employment opportunities will affect not the amount but the
temporal distribution of work. Women will avoid entering the
labor force during periods when they would be subjected to long
and expensive job hunts. The discouraged worker effect represents not a net loss in labor force activity but rather an optimization of its timing. Women who intend to work only 50
percent of the time hunt for jobs when they are easiest rather
than hardest to find. Professor Mincer's optimization hypothesis is intriguing but unproved and perhaps unprovable since appropriate tests cannot be readily devised.

LABOR SUPPLY AND PUBLIC POLICY

The empirical shape of the labor supply function, a matter
only now being thoroughly investigated, has great relevance for
public policy. For example, how progressive should the progressive income tax be? The answer depends on a popular consensus
and also on how taxes affect work decisions. Highly progressive rates might be considered equitable but still be undesirable if the effect on work incentives and output is too unfavorable. The progressive income tax, like any income tax, reduces
the effective after-tax wage—presumably the wage that moti-
vates work decisions. Thus, "do it yourself" is very popular
in England despite the low price of services. Apparently, high
tax rates on market work have led to a substitution in favor of
homework. If the labor supply schedule is positively sloped
throughout, then highly progessive tax rates on upper income
groups will discourage work effort among the most skilled members of the entrepreneurial, administrative, and professional
classes. If the schedule is backward bending, higher taxes
felicitously will encourage more work. To complicate matters
further, short- and long-run effects may be quite different.
Those occupying choice jobs have already undergone the necessary training and may be so pleased with the status, the enjoy-
ability, or the creativity of the work that their efforts are
relatively insensitive to financial rewards. The short-run
supply schedule of labor may be completely inelastic. However,
changes in after-tax wages may significantly affect the occupational choices of future generations.

Similar incentive questions arise when we consider the poverty and welfare problems. There are two schools of thought here. Adherents to the "investment in human capital" approach argue that the working poor are poor because of low productivity. Their problems can be solved most effectively by raising their on-the-job productivity. Investments in education, on-the-job training, and counseling are seen as the route to higher income. Higher productivity will lead to higher wages and permanently raise families above the poverty threshold. On the other hand, proponents of income transfers are concerned that the gestation period for these investments may be quite long. It may be that the present generation of the poor will be only marginally assisted by training programs; the payoff on investments in education will accrue mainly to their children. They argue that the poor are poor because their income is low. If their incomes were raised, they would no longer be poor. The poverty problem can be handled best by direct income transfers that permit the poor to spend their incomes as they see fit, relieve them from oppressive dealings with the welfare bureaucracy, and save the great costs entailed by the existence of this bureaucracy.

Transferring income to the poor is not as simple a process as it might seem. While there are a wide number of income transference schemes under discussion, the most popular proposal is the *negative income tax* (or guaranteed annual income). It was recommended by the President's Commission on Income Maintenance Programs and a complicated variant was proposed to Congress in 1969 by the Nixon administration. The negative income tax can be defined by an annual income guarantee, Y_G, and tax rate, t. The income guarantee and the tax rate determine the program cutoff point, C. Thus, $C = Y_G/t$. All families whose incomes are below the cutoff point will receive some income subsidy. One hypothetical plan advocated by the President's Commission calls for income guarantees of $750 per adult and $450 per child per year, and a tax rate of 50 percent. A family of two adults and two children would be eligible for a guarantee of $2400. All such families earning less than $4800 would be eligible for some benefits ($2400/.50 = $4800). The same size family with zero earnings would receive the guarantee of $2400. A family with earnings of $2000 would receive the $2400 guarantee plus half their earnings for a total of $3400. A family with earnings of $4000 would receive the guarantee plus half their earnings for a total of $4400. The negative income tax raises potential family income while lowering the effective wage rate confronting the family. Consequently, it has a negative income and a negative substitution effect, and must discourage labor input. The desirability of the negative income tax as an antipoverty device depends to an appreciable extent on the size of this reduction in labor input.

Our interest in the magnitude of transfer induced labor supply reductions does not stem simply from an anachronistic concern with the Puritan ethic. The impact of an antipoverty program on work productivity and incentives will be a prime determinant of the program's expense and efficiency. How many persons will reduce their work effort and by how much? To answer these questions, it is first necessary to estimate a labor supply function and to isolate the relationship between wage and income changes and work decisions. The labor supply function can then be employed to simulate labor force withdrawals under alternative negative income tax plans. Thus, a labor supply function of the following form might be estimated for the husband, with the subscript h denoting that the variable refers to the husband and s to his spouse.

$$L_h = aE_h + bE_s + cY_n + dN + eT \qquad (1)$$

where L = the number of manhours of labor market activity
         E = potential wage rate, the wages a person could
               expect to earn given his location and personal
               productivity
         Y_n = family property income
         N = a vector of variables standing for needs, taste,
               and home productivity
         T = transitory influences on income

Once the coefficients a, b, and c are estimated, the impact of the negative income tax can be assessed (assuming there are no alterations in preference structures) by entering its parameters into a labor supply equation as follows:

$$L_h = a(1 - t)E_h + b(1 - t)E_s + c(Y_G - tY_n) + dN + eT \qquad (2)$$

The results of equation (2) are then simulated and subtracted from the results of equation (1).

Although the theory is clear, the art of fitting labor supply functions is still in its infancy. Following the procedures above and using a sample of 50,000 low and medium income persons from the February and March 1966 Current Population Survey, Kalachek and Raines estimated a labor supply function and then simulated the impact of a negative income tax. They estimated that a negative income tax with a $2400 guarantee for a family of four and a 50 percent tax rate would result in labor supply reductions of about 35 percent among males ages 14-62 who were members of families earning $4800 a year or less.[5]

---

[5]"Labor Supply of Low Income Workers," in *Technical Studies*, The President's Commission on Income Maintenance Programs

On the other hand, to cite another interesting recent study,
David H. Greenberg and Marvin Kosters,[6] using the same theoretical model but somewhat different statistical specifications,
estimated a reduction of less than three percent for working
married males under 62 years of age. This huge difference in
results indicates that further and substantial experimentation
and research are required before the labor supply function becomes a trustworthy tool for determining public policy.

THE BACKWARD BENDING LABOR SUPPLY CURVE

Different individuals react to wage changes differently.
For some, higher wages make possible the purchase of deeply
coveted goods such as a larger home in the suburbs or a college education for the children. In such instances, the substitution effect dominates the income effect, and the labor
supply schedule is positively sloped—higher wages induce more
work effort. On the other hand, the dweller in a traditional
village in an underdeveloped country with a highly limited
taste for material goods will find that at higher wages he can

---

[5]cont. (Washington, D.C.: U.S. Government Printing Office,
1970), p. 179; and "Labor Supply and the Negative Income Tax,"
Mimeo, Washington University, 1971. Both income and substitution elasticities were relatively high among lower and lower
middle income groups. For men, a 1.0 percent rise in income,
wages constant, was associated with a .3 percent decline in
annual hours worked. Depending on age, a 1.0 percent decline
in wages, income constant, was associated with a decrease in
annual manhours ranging from .7 percent to 1.0. The substitution elasticity overwhelmed the income elasticity over the
range of consideration, yielding a positively sloped supply
schedule. However, both elasticities declined as income rose.
This suggests that a labor supply function fitted to middle and
upper income families might become more inelastic. A similarly
high degree of responsiveness is found by Sandra S. Christensen,
"Income Maintenance and the Labor Supply" (Ph.D. thesis, University of Wisconsin, 1971).

[6]"Income Guarantees and the Working Poor: The Effect of Income
Maintenance Programs on the Hours of Work of Male Family Heads,"
Rand, R-579-OEO, December 1970. Greenberg and Kosters simulated modest withdrawals because they estimated modest labor
supply responses to economic incentives. Low degrees of response were also found in a number of other studies, including
Michael J. Boskin, "The Economics of the Labor Supply," Stan-
ford University Research Center in Economic Growth Memorandum
No. 110, November 1970.

satisfy his needs with fewer hours of work—the income effect
then dominates. The supply schedule bends backward with higher
wages inducing less effort. Practical observers have long been
aware of the possibility of a backward bending supply curve.
An Englishman of the seventeenth century wrote: "Everyone but
an idiot knows that the lower classes must be kept poor or they
will never be industrious; I do not mean that the poor of England are to be kept like the poor of France but, the states of
the country considered, they must (like all mankind) be in poverty or they will not work."

The slope of the aggregate supply function of labor is
thus a matter for empirical investigation rather than a priori
determination. Still, given the values, taste, and consumption
technology of our society, a backward bending schedule is the
reasonable thing to expect. Leisure and consumption goods are
complements as well as substitutes. It is a mistake to regard
leisure as simply a period of rest, of inactivity, and of passivity.

Gary S. Becker has correctly observed that most consumption activities involve an input of the consumer's time.[7] For
instance, it is too narrow to define a play as "an output dependent on the input of actors, script, and theatre." The unit
of output is more reasonably defined as attending a play, which
involves the input of actors, script, theatre, and the playgo-
er's time. On reflection, the distinction between leisure and
work is not as sharp as it seems at first glance. Utility can
be generated either by working in the market place or home to
secure goods and services, or by combining time with those
goods and services to produce a pleasurable experience. Any
decision to purchase and consume goods and services involves a
concomitant decision to devote time to their consumption. The
income effect involves more than purchasing additional consumption goods and pure leisure or passivity. The changed and augmented mix of consumption goods that accompanies higher levels
of income involves a changed demand for consumption time. Some
consumption goods require modest time input from the consumer;
others demand considerable time (are time intensive). Income
increases normally result in a higher demand for leisure since
more consumption goods require more consumption time. The time
intensity of luxury items is of central importance here. Indeed, higher income would lead to more work if luxury items required little time input, whereas inferior commodities were
time intensive. However, the luxury items people purchase with
higher incomes tend to be quite time intensive. The enjoyment
of boats, swimming pools, snowmobiles, foreign travel, or other

---

[7]"A Theory of the Allocation of Time," *The Economic Journal*,
September 1965, pp. 493-517.

highly income elastic consumption goods clearly requires an appreciable input of consumer time.

The existence of a backward bending labor supply schedule is supported on balance by cross-sectional econometric studies. For instance, using data from the 1950 decennial census, T. Aldrich Finegan estimated that a 1.0 percent rise in wage rates caused a .3 percent decline in hours worked.[8] However, the most powerful support for the existence of a backward bending labor supply schedule comes not from intuition, subtle reasoning, or cross-sectional econometric studies, but from economic history. Over the long sweep of time people have clearly used higher hourly wages to purchase both more consumption goods and the leisure with which to enjoy these consumption goods. Since the end of the nineteenth century, output per person has risen by only two-thirds as much as output per hour. The difference reflects mainly the purchase of additional leisure per person. Those who argue that American society is dominated by the desire to produce and acquire material goods have misinterpreted the technology of consumption and the subtlety of consumer taste. Physical output would be considerably higher today if producers had not chosen to take approximately one-third of their rise in productivity over the past three-quarters of a century in the form of additional leisure.[9] Standard hours of work have been shortened. Holidays and vacations have been lengthened. Retirement occurs earlier. Kreps and Spengler assert:

> Today's worker takes his nonworking time in different forms, but in total he enjoys about 1200 hours per year more free time than did the worker of 1890. Moreover, he enjoys more years in which he doesn't work at all; he enters the labor force much later in life, and has several more years in retirement than his grandfather. In total, this increase at the beginning and the end of work life has given him about nine additional nonworking years.

---

[8]"Hours of Work in the United States: A Cross-Sectional Analysis," *Journal of Political Economy*, October 1962, pp. 452-470.

[9]A note of caution may be useful here since the data may overstate the backward bending slope of the supply schedule. Shorter hours may to some extent be offset by longer commuting times and by a greater intensity of input. It is clear that people in industrialized but less affluent lands work longer hours than do Americans, but it is also clear that they work at a somewhat more leisurely pace.

Kreps and Spengler categorize the sources of increased annual leisure between 1890 and 1963 as follows: shorter work week—1100 hours, paid holidays—32 hours, paid vacations—48 hours, and paid sick leaves—40 hours.[10] Before 1940, the shortened standard work week accounted for most of the reduction in average hours worked. Since then, there has been a decided trend toward a 40 hour week in activities like trade, services, and transportation, in which hours had been considerably longer. As yet, with a few dramatic exceptions, there appears little inclination to reduce the standard work week below 40 hours. The modern trend toward more leisure is expressing itself in the form of earlier retirements and longer vacations, holidays, and other paid time off.

At first glance, Table 1 suggests that the labor force participation rate has been immune from the otherwise powerful movement toward a more leisure oriented society. The labor force has shown some fluctuation but virtually no trend change. Indeed, if there has been any trend, it has been toward more participation. A closer look at Table 1 indicates that this historic stability is the result of offsetting trends among different age-sex groups. An analysis of the behavior of these age-sex groups casts doubt on our first impressions. The stability of the participation rate appears to be simply a statistical artifact, concealing a great reduction in the amount of nonmarket work performed by women.

Participation among adult males in the prime working ages of 25-44 has been very high and relatively constant over time. Men in this age category work fewer hours per week and fewer weeks per year than was once considered normal, but virtually all still work. Interesting social and economic trends have affected older men, younger boys, and women (particularly married women). All these trends are compatible with the purchase of larger amounts of leisure per year and the increase in the number of years spent outside the labor force. They point both to the complex fashion in which the family unit utilizes higher productivity to purchase additional leisure, and to the effect of social legislation on work decisions.

The beneficent operation of the income effect has dominated the labor force behavior of older men. The participation rate of men past age 65 has fallen steadily and sharply. Only one-fourth of such men are now working, as compared with almost two-thirds at the beginning of the century. Participation among men between the ages of 45 and 64 is also beginning to

---

[10]Juanita M. Kreps and Joseph H. Spengler, "The Leisure Component of Economic Growth" in *Automation and Economic Progress*, eds., Howard R. Bowen and Garth L. Mangum (Englewood Cliffs, New Jersey: Prentice-Hall, Inc., 1966), pp. 128-134.

Table 1.   *Labor Force Participation Rates by Age and Sex, 1890–1970**
(Percent)

		Male					
Year	Total Labor Force (Age 14 and over)	Total (Age 14 and over)	14–19	20–24	25–44	45–64	65 and over
1890	52	84	50	91	96	96	68
1900	54	86	62	91	95	95	63
1920	54	85	52	90	96	96	56
1930	53	82	40	89	96	96	54
1940	53	80	35	88	93	96	42
1950	54	79	40	82	98	93	42
1960	55	77	38	86	95	89	31
	Total Labor Force (Age 16 and over)	Total (Age 16 and over)	16–19	20–24	25–44	45–64	65 and over
1960Ψ	60	84	59	90	98	92	33
1970Ψ	61	81	58	87	97	89	27

		Female					
		Total (Age 14 and over)	14–19	20–24	25–44	45–64	65 and over	Married, husband present
1890		18	25	30	15	12	8	5
1900		20	27	32	18	14	8	
1920		23	28	38	22	17	8	
1930		24	23	42	25	18	8	
1940		26	19	46	31	20	6	15
1950		29	23	43	33	29	8	22
1960		34	24	45	39	42	11	31
		Total (Age 16 and over)	16–19	20–24	25–44	45–64	65 and over	
1960Ψ		38	27	46	40	44	11	
1970Ψ		44	44	58	48	49	10	

Sources: 1890–1950 U. S. Department of Commerce, Bureau of the Census, *Historical Statistics of the United States, Colonial Times to 1957,* p. 71.

1960 U. S. Department of Commerce, Bureau of the Census, *U. S. Census of Population, 1960: General Social and Economic Characteristics, U. S. Summary,* pp. I-213 and I-214.

1960Ψ U. S. Department of Labor, Bureau of Labor Statistics, "Employment and Unemployment in 1960," Special Labor Force Report No. 14, pp. A-13 and A-15.

1970Ψ "Employment and Unemployment in 1970," Special Labor Force Report No. 129, pp. A-7 and A-8.

*Data for 1890–1960 are from the decennial census. Data for 1960Ψ and 1970Ψ are annual averages of the monthly estimates of the Current Population Survey and are not directly comparable with decennial census data.

decline as the age of retirement lowers. Between 1950 and 1970
the number of retired workers receiving Social Security benefits rose from 1.7 to 13.3 million. The average monthly payment in 1970 purchasing power rose from $70 to $118. The
number of persons covered by private pension plans rose from 10
to 29 million and the number of beneficiaries from .5 to 4 million.[11] Between them, Social Security and private pension
plans increasingly have allowed the old to receive income without working. They have quite reasonably responded by not working.
     Still, all of the reduction in participation is not volun-
tary. In earlier times, many employers would keep aging workers on the payroll partially from a feeling of obligation and
partially because the knowledge of former employees living in
destitution did not contribute to the morale or loyalty of current employees. Social Security and private pension plans
changed all this. Employers regard these programs as fulfill-
ing their moral obligation to long service employees. These
obligations met, they have instituted compulsory retirement to
replace aging employees whose energy is lagging and whose
skills may be obsolete with younger workers. If this were
still a country of small farms and businesses, more old people
would be working. The self-employed are less prone to early
retirement than are wage and salary workers. Rather than re-
tiring abruptly at some arbitrary age, the self-employed gradually reduce hours and intensity of input. This suggests that
some portion of the decline in labor effort by the old (resulting from Social Security and pension plans) is involuntary and
socially undesirable. However, the desire for retirement of
wage and salary workers is undoubtedly greater than that of the
self-employed, since they must meet work standards and schedules set by others, and cannot control their own intensity of
effort.
     Work opportunities for teenagers have been eroded by the
decline of the family business, which was content with the efficiency of teenage labor paid zero wages, and by laws requiring school attendance and restricting the use of teenagers in
manufacturing and construction. As with old-age pensions, the
motivations underlying social legislation for teenagers were a
mixture of humanitarianism and a desire to reduce competition
in the job market. This narrowing of opportunities represents
only part of the story. Teenagers have benefited considerably
from the higher earnings of their parents. Higher adult wages
have been used to purchase more leisure for children, as well

---

[11]U.S. Bureau of the Census, *Statistical Abstract of the United
States: 1971* (92nd edition), Washington, D.C., 1971, pp. 278
and 285.

as more years of school attendance. Since school attendance is
an economic activity that raises productivity in subsequent
years, a significant portion of the decline in teenage participation simply represents a shift from market to nonmarket work.
     Declining participation in the labor force among male teen-
agers and older men has been fully offset by rising participation among women. Social mores and family patterns of living
have been revolutionized as the working woman evolved from the
exception to the commonplace. The emergence of the working
wife seems a paradox. We have seen that higher income is
strongly associated with increased leisure. It is well established that the wives of prosperous men are less likely to work
than the wives of poorer men. The real income of husbands has
risen over time. How, then, can we explain the rising participation rates of their wives? The reconciliation is straightforward once we allow for all the relevant facts. We can ex-
press the factors affecting the participation of married women
in a simplified form of our labor supply equation:

$$M = aY + bW + cH \qquad (3)$$

where M = labor force participation of married women
      Y = potential earnings of the husband
      W = wife's wage rate
      H = wife's home marginal productivity

     Statistical studies indicate that b, the coefficient of
the wife's wage, is strongly positive. Among married women,
the substitution effect of a wage increase overwhelms the income effect. Powerful substitution effects for married women
are not surprising. The more and the better the alternative
uses of one's time outside the market place, the higher should
be the substitution effect. The positive coefficient b is substantially larger than a, the negative coefficient for the husband's income. The secular increase in men's income, Y, which
discourages participation, has been paralleled by an equivalent
rise in women's wage rates, W, which encourages participation.
The labor force participation rate of married women has risen
because their positive response to their own wage rate advances
has swamped their negative response to advances in the wage
rates of their husbands.[12]
     Perhaps even more important, there has been a substantial
decline in H, home marginal productivity, occurring along with

---

[12]See Jacob Mincer, "Labor Force Participation of Married
Women," in *Aspects of Labor Economics*, National Bureau of Eco-
nomic Research (Princeton, New Jersey: Princeton University
Press, 1962), pp. 63-97.

a substantial increase in home average productivity—output per hour. The continuing technical revolution has had at least as pronounced an effect on working conditions in the household as in the factory. The proliferation of capital equipment in the household—washer, dryer, dishwasher, garbage disposal, electric can opener, vacuum cleaner, freezer, larger refrigerator, and the host of small cooking and cleaning appliances has been imposing. In addition, convenience foods, the growing popularity of restaurants and nursery schools, and the use of household materials that require less cleaning and maintenance have increasingly transferred functions from the household to the commercial sector. With smaller family size, the marginal productivity of the housewife working in the home has been reduced. Household tasks that represented a full-time job some decades ago can now be accomplished in an appreciably shorter period. The subtlety of the reasoning here is worth noting. Given the decline in the desired size of the average family, the demand for home products has grown at a modest rate. The amount of output a woman can produce in any hour has grown dramatically. Hence, her productivity between, say the thirtieth and the fortieth hour of work per week is now lower than it once was, since she is able in the initial hours of work to complete more of the high priority, high value production tasks. Time has been released for additional types of homework such as gourmet cooking, chauffeuring, and more intensive child care. Time has also been released for more leisure and for more market work. Increased labor force participation by married women primarily reflects a shift from home to market work. This shift has undoubtedly been associated with an increase rather than a reduction in the amount of leisure.

CONCLUSIONS

The theory of labor supply postulates that the work decisions of family members are determined by the potential wage rates confronting them in the market place, by their income from nonwork related sources, by their relative home productivities, by need and financial obligation, and by their tastes for leisure and for goods and services. The response to higher wages can be decomposed into a substitution effect that encourages additional effort as wages rise and an income effect that discourages work.

Empirical investigations of labor supply involve innumerable difficulties since: (1) The manner in which the official statistics are defined obscures the link between effort and economic incentives. (2) Much effort takes place outside the market place where it is not easily measured. (3) Tastes for goods and for leisure vary considerably between people and also

vary possibly over time. These taste differences cannot be
readily controlled in statistical studies. Despite these difficulties, the relationship between effort and incentive has
been investigated both by rigorous statistical techniques and
by casual historical inspection. Studies conducted to date
suggest that the cross-sectional labor supply schedule is positively sloped in the low and medium wage range and then bends
backward in the higher wage range. However, rigorous statistical investigation of the cross-sectional supply schedule is
still in its infancy and little definitive information is
available. Historically, the matter is far more straightforward. Over time, the supply schedule has shown a very decided
backward bend. Advances in technology, health, education, and
the size of the capital stock have led to substantially higher
real wages. The average family has taken two-thirds of the
benefits in the form of more goods and services and one-third
in the form of more leisure with which to enjoy this augmented
affluence.

3

The Quality of Labor

It is commonplace that some workers contribute more to
output and receive higher compensation than do others. Neuro-
surgeons, research physicists, and plant managers are more
highly productive and more highly paid than unskilled workers.
Sharp interpersonal differences exist even within the confines
of a single occupation. Given the same availability of cooper-
ating factors, some workers can and do produce more than
others. Substitute Mr. Jones for Mr. Smith, holding all other
things constant, and output will rise. Further, some workers
possess greater versatility. They can operate efficiently
throughout a range of activities in their chosen occupations.
Others are proficient only in narrow subspecialties.
  Some of these qualitative differences are traceable to
the vagaries of genetic endowment and to the vicissitudes surrounding the development of human personalities. Some reflect
the results of prior investments in human capital. Human productive capability is partially the result of natural endowment—what we will call *raw labor*. Partially it is a produced
good, just as computers, lathes, and other items of physical
capital are produced goods. It is questionable whether workers
are paid their marginal product, but there is little doubt that
there is a strong correlation between productivity and compensation. Interpersonal differences in wages can thus also be
viewed as largely reflecting interpersonal differences in raw
labor and in investments in human capital. These investments
include expenditures on child rearing, nutrition, health, education, and training. They also include expenditures on securing information about where one's capabilities can be most
efficiently utilized and expenditures on geographic mobility.
  Workers can be viewed as capitalists whose major asset is
investment in themselves. This human capital perspective has
often been slighted because education, health, and other human
investments have major consumption components and are also
areas of social and humanitarian concern. Many believe, and

31

quite legitimately so, that we should allocate more resources
to human development because it is the right thing to do. Be-
lieving that man is the measure of all things, they are re-
pelled by the concept of man as an input into the productive
process and protest efforts to find the rate of return on human
capital. Still, we shall never adequately comprehend the operation of the labor market or establish rational social welfare or growth programs until we recognize the influence of
investment in human capital on individual productivity. Further, like other important insights, the concept of human capital, once enunciated, seems self-evident. Health, literacy,
and training clearly do contribute to productivity.

The effectiveness of the labor supply can be augmented by
investments in people. How far should this process be carried?[1]
The traditional theory of investment in physical capital is an
appropriate starting point for this discussion. Investment is
simply an abstinence from current consumption that permits resources to be organized in a form that raises future productive
capacity. The current abstinence represents the cost of the
investment. The augmentation of future productivity and income
represents the return. The first step in determining the desirability of any investment is to solve for the internal rate
of return. This is the discount rate that equates future expected proceeds with current costs; it is the annual rate of
return on cost. A dollar earned today is worth more than a
dollar earned tomorrow. Today's dollar can provide either immediate consumption satisfaction or can earn more income by
being invested at a positive rate of interest. Consequently,
this discounting process properly attributes less value to a
dollar earned in the far future than to a dollar earned in the
immediate future.

$$\sum_{t=0}^{n} \frac{C_t}{(1 + r)t} = \sum_{t=0}^{n} \frac{R_t}{(1 + r)t} \tag{1}$$

where C = cost of investment
  R = additional revenues resulting from the investment
  r = internal rate of return
  t = time

---

[1]For a fuller treatment of the intricate and important subject
of human capital creation, see a companion volume in the Wadsworth Series in Labor Economics and Industrial Relations:
Lester Thurow, *Investment in Human Capital* (Belmont, California:
Wadsworth Publishing Company, Inc., 1970).

The advisability of an investment yielding a positive return can be determined only by comparison with its alternatives. In a world of perfect certainty, investors in physical capital would undertake in sequential order of profitability all investments whose internal rate of return equaled or exceeded the interest rate at which funds could be borrowed or lent.[2] Investments yielding an eight percent return would be worthwhile if the market interest rate were five percent but not if it were ten percent. The future is, however, far from perfectly certain. Interest payments on high grade securities may be a very safe proposition, but the outcome of any specific investment in physical capital is shrouded in uncertainty. Consumer tastes may change, technical advance may make the product obsolete, or competitors may flood the market with good substitutes. The investor in physical capital will consequently insist on an internal rate of return sufficiently higher than the interest rate to compensate him for this uncertainty. The investor in human capital is even more plagued by the inability to discern clearly the flow of revenues that will result from his actions. The returns from a college education depend importantly on the economic ability of the student, a subject on which the investor's knowledge may be quite limited. Further, the returns are spread over a 40-year time span. Demands may alter greatly over time, as the aerospace engineering graduates of the early 1960s discovered during the recession of the late 1960s and early 1970s.

If the investor in human capital were a slave owner, he would proceed in precisely the same fashion as would the investor in physical capital. He would undertake in sequential order of their attractiveness all investments in nutrition, health, education, training, search, and mobility, whose internal rate of return exceeded or equaled the interest rate plus the premium required for bearing the uncertainty. The private investor in human capital is, however, not a slave owner investing in others. He is a free man allocating resources to his own development or to that of a close relative. His focus will consequently be different. He will consider not only the revenues and costs associated with an investment act but also the consumption consequences of the act. A potential college student proceeding in a rational manner should consider not

---

[2] The internal rate of return is widely used in the literature on human capital and has the virtue of permitting convenient comparisons between the profitability of investments in human and other forms of capital. An alternative approach, the calculation of net present values is, however, somewhat preferable when actually making investment decisions. See Lester Thurow, *Investment in Human Capital*, Chapter 2.

only the costs of going to college and its subsequent effect on income, he should also consider the pleasurableness or strain of college attendance, the influence of college on his personality—on his ability to enjoy the world—and the nonmonetary advantages or disadvantages of the job options provided by a college education.

Investments in human capital are undertaken both by individuals and by society. In many instances, the costs are shared. These partners will view the attractiveness of an investment differently. The individual will be concerned only with the private rate of return. He will consider only the costs that he bears and the benefits that he receives. In the case of income benefits, he will consider only the after-tax increment in income. Since the variability in return to investment in human capital is high, so will be his uncertainty premium. Since human capital is poor collateral, the individual coming from a low income family will be able to borrow only at high interest rates and so will undertake investments only if they seem to offer high rates of return. Society's view is necessarily broader. For society, cost includes all real resources devoted to the investment, not simply private resources. Its computation of benefits will include all gains in output, not simply those that can be privately appropriated. Society will be interested in pre-tax rather than after-tax increments in private income. It will be concerned with externalities, with gains or losses that accrue to individuals other than those in whom the investment is being made. Since uncertainty is less serious for the mass than for the individual, society will have a lower uncertainty premium. Taking account of these factors, social rates of return may differ substantially from private rates. Further, society has a better credit rating and hence will utilize a lower interest rate for comparison purposes. It is not surprising, then, that society may frequently find it expedient to bear some portion of the costs of investments which are more profitable to it than they are to the individual. The alternative outcome, a private rate of return higher than the social rate of return, is also feasible. A college education may, for instance, enable an individual to secure a higher paying job though he may be no more productive on that job than the less well-educated person who would otherwise occupy it.

THE PRIVATE RATE OF RETURN ON HIGHER EDUCATION

At least up to some point, investments in nutrition and in health obviously have a significant impact on work capability. The precise magnitude of this impact, the rate of return on investments in nutrition and health, may not really be a matter

of great interest or importance. The prevention, cure, or al-
leviation of cancer, heart disease, or mental illness excites
us more for its immediate effects than for its investment aspect. We are far more concerned with reducing anguish and increasing the length and joyfulness of life than with the gains
in output that would accompany a longer-lived and healthier
population. Education is a more complex matter. Individual
self-development and the proper fulfillment of one's role as a
citizen in a democratic society are powerful arguments for an
educated population. Still, they tell us little about how much
and what type of education are desirable. The liberating and
consumption aspects of education are important, but few would
regard them as adequate justification for the current magnitude
of our investment in the school system. Information on rates
of return to investment are necessary to guide both individual
and social decision making in the realm of education.

It will be worthwhile to examine some of the statistical
evidence on the rate of return to investment in education. We
will concentrate on the private rate of return, since it has
been studied more comprehensively and convincingly than the social rate of return. The statistical studies here certainly
support the theory that education significantly affects the
productive ability and income earning capability of the average
individual. At the same time, these studies also show how pre-
carious and roundabout is our knowledge in this important area.

Gary S. Becker,[3] using data from the 1950 decennial census,
attempted to estimate expected private rates of return for college attendance to 1949 college graduates. The expected future
rate of return is clearly the rate of return relevant for students contemplating additional schooling and for the government,
which needs quantitative guidance in allocating its investment
dollars between education, research, and physical capital. Unfortunately, this relevant rate of return can never be known
with any assurance. The rate of return that will be earned by
today's students will be knowable only after they have all completed their working careers and died or retired. To proceed
at all, we must find a proxy for this future time series. This
problem is coped with by assuming that today's college graduates, when they reach 40, 50, or 60 years of age, will have the
same earning advantage, as compared with high school graduates,
as is possessed by college graduates who currently are 40, 50,
or 60 years old. The expected rate of return for today's group
of students is thus estimated as a weighted average of rates of
return for preceding groups. Such a procedure is inherently
deficient since we know that the future will not recapitulate

---

[3]Gary S. Becker, *Human Capital* (New York: National Bureau of
Economic Research, 1964).

the past. (1) The economic advantage of today's 60-year-old
college graduate reflects the scarcity value of education in
his own group rather than the scarcity value for today's graduate. (2) A year of education in 1930 is not the same as a year
of education in 1970. The quantity and type of information
taught in a school year will vary as knowledge and educational
technology alter. (3) The relative abilities of high school
and college graduates will vary between generations. (4) Over
time, economic growth will raise the real income of both college and high school graduates.

No one has devised a satisfactory adjustment for the first
three distortions. Becker and others attempt to adjust for the
continuing process of economic growth by extrapolating past
rates of growth in real income (after making an allowance for
that fraction of past growth attributable to increased educational attainment). The after-tax income of high school graduates is then subtracted from the after-tax income of college
graduates for each age group of graduates to obtain an earnings
differential. This differential is scaled downward to adjust
for death rates. The economic benefits of education come later
in life and all do not survive to receive them. Even those who
survive must recognize that the costs of education are borne in
one's youth and the benefits reaped only subsequently. Private
costs are the sum of private educational outlays and private
foregone earnings. Educational outlays consist of expenditures
for books, tuition, and fees. Foregone earnings are the difference between the earnings of a student attending college and
the earnings achievable had he been working full time. Even
for students attending private schools, foregone earnings are
considerably more important than educational outlays. Once the
time profile of costs and benefits is estimated, the formula
shown in equation (1) can be used to solve for the internal
rate of return on college education.

We cannot directly observe the effects of education on the
productive capability and earnings potential of a single individual. Rather, we must make comparisons between persons with
more and less education. Interpreting internal rates of return
would be relatively straightforward if people differed only in
years of schooling. However, people with different educational
attainment also show race, sex, location, and family background
differences. These differences must be controlled for to the
largest extent feasible, lest we attribute to education income
benefits that are actually derived from some other personal
characteristic. Becker attempted to cope with this problem by
conducting his analysis for such relatively homogeneous groups
as urban native-born white males. For this group, Becker estimates the internal rate of return on college education at 13
percent. For other groups, such as women and blacks, the rate
of return was smaller but still not inconsiderable. The rate

of return on high school attendance and graduation was also
computed and was quite substantial at 20 percent. Other studies have yielded somewhat different results, but all American
studies have shown quite handsome rates of return to investment
in education. Thus, Giora Hanoch, using 1960 census data, a
more elaborate set of statistical controls, and treating foregone earnings as the only school cost, found a 17 percent rate
of return on high school graduation and a 10 percent rate of
return on college graduation for white males.[4] A small scale
panel study of the impact of post high school technical education on income in the years immediately following education
suggested an internal rate of return of 16.5 percent.[5]

Of course, it is not sufficient to control only for race,
sex, location, and the grosser aspects of family background.
The students who receive the most education tend to have above
average ability and a family background that contributes to a
successful career. Could it be that the benefits attributed
to education are really derived from (are proxy for) these
other success generating characteristics? Do persons with more
education receive higher incomes primarily because education is
economically productive or primarily because they are abler individuals? Investigators of this crucial question are handi-
capped since economic ability cannot readily be defined in a
nontautological fashion, and since the available data measure
ability imperfectly. Scores on I.Q. or other intelligence
tests or rank in high school graduating class are normally
used as measures for ability. Persons attending the same high
school and graduating in the top fifth of their class or persons with approximately the same I.Q. might be treated as
having comparable abilities. Having grouped individuals in
this fashion, differences in earnings between those who went on
to college and those who did not would be attributed solely to
education. Findings to date include the following: If controls
for ability are introduced, education still has a powerful effect on earnings. Becker concluded that "even after adjustment
for differential ability, the private rate of return to a typical white male college graduate would be considerable, say,
certainly more than 10 percent."[6] On the other hand, education
and ability do interact powerfully. Abler persons secure far
more benefits from additional years of schooling than do the

---

[4]"An Economic Analysis of Earnings and Schooling," *The Journal
of Human Resources*, Number 3, Summer 1967, p. 322.

[5]Adger B. Carroll and Loren A. Ihmen, "Costs and Returns for
Two Years of Post-secondary Technical Schooling: A Pilot
Study," *The Journal of Political Economy*, December 1967, p. 868.

[6]*Human Capital*, p. 88.

less able. Indeed, there is serious question as to whether
higher education would be economically advantageous for the
less capable portion of the population.[7]

In the past, higher education was reserved mainly for the
more capable. There seems little doubt that higher education
was a highly profitable undertaking both for students and for
society, yielding an average rate of return at least comparable
to that of corporate manufacturing investment. This profitability has encouraged a major expansion in school attendance.
The percent of 16- and 17-year-olds enrolled in school rose
from 71 percent in 1950 to 83 percent in 1960, and to 90 percent in 1970. The percent of 18- and 19-year-olds enrolled
rose from 29 to 38 to 48 percent for the same years. Most
dramatically, the percent of 20- to 24-year-olds rose from 9 to
13 to 22 percent also for the same years.[8] Is this expansion
warranted? Should everyone contemplate at least four years of
college? There is serious need for caution here. The laws of
supply and demand and of diminishing returns apply to education
as well as to other inputs. The economic productivity of higher education should decline as more and more persons acquire
college degrees. Unless there is an acceleration of technical
change leading to a greatly enhanced demand for educated workers, the marginal productivity of education may drop dramatically in the next decade. Further, increasing enrollment rates
are changing the quality of college students. Diminishing returns aside, the average college graduate of the 1970s can expect a lower rate of return on his investment than the average
college graduate of the 1950s and 1960s, simply because he is—
on the average—less capable.

Even at rates of return lower than those prevailing in the
past, higher education may remain a good investment. However,
this does not mean that it will be highly desirable for every
individual. The student who completes his formal education
with or prior to high school graduation is not necessarily act-
ing irrationally. He should not be treated as a social leper.
We assume the typical individual to be a utility rather than an
income maximizer. He consequently must consider nonpecuniary
advantages and disadvantages, as well as rates of return. Education is highly enjoyable and enriching for some, but a source
of considerable frustration for others. The less interested
·and the less educationally capable may find lower paying jobs

---

[7]W. Lee Hansen, Burton A. Weisbrod, and William J. Scanlon,
"Schooling and Learning of Low Achievers," *American Economic
Review*, June 1970.

[8]U.S. Department of Commerce, Bureau of the Census, *Statistical
Abstract of the United States*, 1971 (Washington, D.C.: U.S.
Government Printing Office, 1971), p. 105.

easier to endure than years of unpleasant schooling. Also, the
costs of schooling occur now; the financial benefits come in
later life. The rate of time preference for some may exceed
the rate of return on education. The higher current consumption associated with entering the labor market on a full-time
basis may rationally be preferred to the higher future consumption associated with obtaining a high school degree or a college education.

Finally, the economic benefits of education depend on
ability and luck. The average rate of return on a college education is high, but so is the dispersion around this average.
The 13 percent rate of return reported by Becker was an average,
including some who reaped much larger profits and some who
earned zero or even negative returns. A recent study of lower
income workers indicated that each additional year of education
added only five cents to their rate of hourly earnings, a tri-
fling return indeed.[9] For some people, additional education is
simply a poor investment. This minority of disappointed investors will surely grow in size as the educational attainment of
the population continues to rise.

KNOWLEDGE AND PRODUCTION

Why and how does education contribute to productivity and
income? In some instances, the answer is straightforward. Important components of the educational system are job oriented.
They impart the knowledge and skills required to perform adequately certain types of work. A number of important vocational skills are taught in some high schools. Technical skills
are increasingly emphasized in the growing number of community
or two-year colleges. The specialized knowledge necessary or
advantageous for more complex jobs is frequently taught in professional or graduate schools. Colleges of medicine, law,
journalism, architecture, social work, and engineering, and the
graduate departments in the natural and social sciences are all
centers for job training.

Specialized training is, however, not the major thrust of
the American educational system. Most high school graduates
are not adequately trained for a vocational career. Most college graduates receive a general education and do not go on to
specialized postgraduate work. How does such an education
build human capital? Why should four years of psychology, so-
ciology, economics, mathematics, and art appreciation substan-

---

[9] Edward D. Kalachek and Fredric Q. Raines, "The Labor Supply of
Low Income Workers," in *Technical Studies*, The President's Commission on Income Maintenance Programs, pp. 182-185.

tially affect subsequent labor market productivity? Some
scholars question whether it does. They doubt the contribution
of advanced, nonprofessional education to a society's economic
potential. These skeptics reason that the educational system
simply serves as a screening device for employers. Employers
are aware that abler people normally secure more education.
Further, acquiring a high school or college degree demonstrates
the existence of some personal ambition, motivation, and self-
discipline. It indicates the capability for responding to institutional restrictions and incentives. At going wage rates,
employers will consequently prefer more to less well-educated
workers. More educated workers will be hired for the better
paying jobs. As larger numbers of workers obtain higher education, employers can insist on more exalted educational credentials for more and more jobs. Rising levels of education thus
result in the more educated preempting more and more of the
desirable jobs, pushing the less educated down into lower paying activities. For the average individual, more education is
economically desirable since it increases the probability of
obtaining a preferred job. Social benefits are another matter.
They exist, if at all, only because education has consumption
attributes or contributes to better citizenship. There is no
evidence that the educational system turns out more productive
or better qualified workers.[10]

These views cannot be rejected out of hand. Some individuals do obtain preferred jobs because of educational credentials even though these credentials have not significantly enhanced their productivity. Further, detailed knowledge on how
general education enters into the production function is simply
nonexistent. There are no convincing simulations of how an increment of education affects individual productivity. Still,
informal observation and an appreciation of the needs of technology have convinced most scholars that income differences
between educational classes primarily represent returns to investment in human capital. Education seems to impart the
ability to learn rapidly in new environments and to cope with
new problems. The economic function of general education is to
impart general purpose skills, relations, data, and language.
In the cases of reading, writing, and mathematics, this is obvious. Training in many of the natural and social sciences and

---

[10]See, for instance, Barry Anderson and Boyd Morros, "School
and the Labor Force" (Mimeo., Graduate Institute of Education,
Washington University, 1972); Ivar Berg, *Education and Jobs:
The Great Training Robbery* (New York: Praeger Publishers,
1970); and Gary Fields, "A Theory of Education and Labor Markets in Less Developed Countries" (Ph.D. dissertation, University of Michigan, 1972).

in some of the humanities may also create valuable knowledge reservoirs and develop analytic skills. The relationship between educational background and work competence was succinctly stated by a manufacturer testifying before a British Parliamentary hearing conducted in 1840:

> As men of business or of general usefulness and as men with whom an employer would best like to be surrounded I should, however, decidedly prefer the Saxons and Swiss . . . because they have had a very careful general education, which has extended their capacities beyond any general employment, and rendered them fit to take up, after a short preparation, any employment to which they may be called. If I have an English workman engaged in the erection of a steam engine, he will understand that and nothing else; he will understand only his steam engine, and for other circumstances, or other branches of mechanics, however closely allied, he will be comparatively helpless to adapt himself to all the circumstances that may arise, to make arrangements for them, and to give sound advice or write clear statements and letters on his works in the various related branches of mechanics.[11]

The economic utility of general education depends on the importance of new learning situations. General education would have little economic utility if job content were simple and invariant over time, or if individual workers remained wedded to particular jobs.[12] A self-contained training program could then be constructed for every job. Suppose that a housewife devoted her productive career to preparing six different meals. There would be little economic justification for teaching her to read or write, count or measure. There would be no need for such roundabout and expensive excursions. The recipes could be

---

[11]"Evidence of Employers of Labourers on the Influence of Training and Education on the Value of Workmen, and on the Comparative Eligibility of Educated and Uneducated Workmen for Employment" (Printed by W. Clowes and Sons for Her Majesty's Stationery Office, London, 1840.) Quoted in Mary Jean Bowman, "From Guild to Infant Training Industries" in *Education and Economic Development*, eds., C. Arnold Anderson and Mary Jean Bowman (Chicago: Aldine Publishing Company, 1965), p. 105.

[12]This discussion draws heavily on Richard R. Nelson, Merton J. Peck, and Edward D. Kalachek, *Technology, Economic Growth and Public Policy* (Washington, D.C.: The Brookings Institution, 1967).

taught by an apprenticeship of watching and imitating. On the other hand, apprenticeship is inefficient if the housewife is expected to work with a large and continually changing set of recipes. General education then comes into its own since it permits the housewife to learn rapidly from a cookbook. Within limits, the more extensive the education, the more rapidly a new recipe can be taught. It greatly simplifies matters if a cake recipe can simply state "pour in a cup of milk" and not explain what milk is or describe how to measure and pour. This principle can be generalized readily to all production processes.

The frequency with which people are challenged to learn rapidly in a new situation depends on the extent to which job content varies over time. In turn, this depends on the pace of technical change. In a world in which production and distribution techniques were routinized and stabilized, authentically new learning experiences would be rare. New technology creates premiums throughout the labor force for an education significantly broader than that required for a specific job. The need extends far beyond the skilled and imaginative scientists, engineers, and craftsmen required for the innovation. For an innovation to be rapidly brought to market, there is a need for plant managers and work forces capable of learning to produce the new product. It is not that new technology is inherently more complex; it is simply different. Workers must be able to learn new techniques rapidly and to work with unroutinized processes. Well-educated workers are particularly valuable when job composition changes, since they can be trained relatively easily for a variety of jobs. Thus, during the early days of the transistor industry, highly paid chemical engineers were assigned to production jobs because the jobs were not yet sufficiently routinized to permit the rapid training of workers who lacked technical backgrounds. Salespeople are required who are capable of understanding the properties of the new product sufficiently well to be able to communicate its advantages to their customers. There will be a need for maintenance men capable of learning servicing procedures. The need for managers and workers sufficiently well-trained to evaluate new alternatives and to deal effectively with the problems generated by new products or processes extends beyond the innovating industry. If the innovation is a capital good or an intermediate output, customers will have to be sufficiently sophisticated to absorb it into their own production processes.

Education and technical change are involved in a dynamic cumulative process. Educated and creative people generate technical change, while technical change generates a need for educated people. The great increase in the relative supply of educated people in recent decades would have led us to expect a sharp diminution in the economic rewards given to education.

Instead, rates of return on high school education appear to
have risen sharply, while rates of return on college education
have remained comparatively stable. The increase in supply of
educated personnel was fully offset by an increase in demand
for their services. The augmentation of demand appears partially traceable to feedback effects—a larger class of technically educated persons leading to a more rapid rate of technical change—and partially traceable to the growth of the
health, education, and defense industries. The continuing increase in educational attainment need not lead us into Malthu-
sian pessimism over the rate of return on education. If sufficient funds are allocated to research, the more educated population of the future may generate a rate of technical change
sufficiently rapid to maintain a high economic value, for education.
     The specialized training given within the educational sys-
tem, if of high quality, places great stresses on the ability
to learn rapidly. The training received by an economist in a
good graduate school, for instance, involves only a limited
concentration on his subfield of specialization. Rather, the
heaviest emphasis is placed on theory and statistics, knowledge of which will enable the student to master any subspe-
cialty within a limited time. An education containing large
elements of generality is a roundabout and time-consuming way
to train a practicing economist or electrical engineer. But
the learning ability it imparts provides both versatility and
protection against obsolescence.
     Though necessarily limited, the protection against obso-
lescence is real and important. Schools may be able to do a
better job than they are currently doing in educating for the
jobs of tomorrow, but since the future cannot be known with any
precision, they will never be able to provide the mix of knowledge that students would consider optimum 30 years after graduation. A technically progressive society by its very nature
can never hope to have a labor force optimally suited to its
current needs. Many workers, by the time they reach their
forties or fifties, will be somewhat obsolete, although the
more general their education the less the likelihood of obsolescence. The problem arises because technical knowledge is
embodied mainly in the minds of people who are currently involved in the educational system. As new basic knowledge and
new techniques become more fully understood, they are simplified, formalized, codified, and introduced into the existing
school curriculum. Since the stock of knowledge is continually
increasing, recent school graduates are technically superior to
their predecessors. Earlier generations were not trained with
this knowledge or technique since it did not exist, or its relevance was not yet realized. Rapid technical change is revers-
ing the roles of the young and the old. In the past, when

technical change was slower and knowledge was acquired through experience, the old had the advantage of wisdom. Now, time renders much past education and experience obsolete, whereas the young have the advantage of a more recent and superior education.

ON-THE-JOB TRAINING

All training does not occur in the formal school system. An appreciable amount of specialized knowledge is learned on the job. The formal educational process is costly. So is training at the work site. Training costs are apparent when the employer provides formal lecture rooms, equipment, supplies, and instructors. The more informal training that occurs when workers learn by doing also involves costs. In any operation in which experience has value, the new employee will produce fewer units of an output of given quality than will a more experienced employee. Training thus lowers the receipts and raises the expenditures of an employer during the training interval.

Why do employers provide training?[13] Do they pay for it? If so, why? What determines the distribution of effort between the school system and industry? Employers provide some types of training because it is impossible for them to do otherwise. Universities hiring assistant professors who have no prior teaching experience cannot avoid providing the learning experience that comes from teaching a class for the first time. Other training is provided because it is necessary for the productive process and cannot be acquired elsewhere. Some knowledge is of recent vintage. It is not yet adequately understood or sufficiently routinized to be incorporated into school curricula. Some knowledge is too specialized to particular production processes to justify teaching it outside the confines of a few firms. Some knowledge is basically informal; it is not sufficiently well understood that it can be acquired except through experience.

More generally, the division of educational labor between employers and the formal educational system is determined by the possibility of capturing the fruits of the training. A firm that bears the cost of training its employees will be paying a higher wage than the worker's productivity during the training period justifies. A profit maximizing firm will be willing to lose money on its employees during the training

---

[13]The framework for analyzing on-the-job training is developed in Gary S. Becker, *Human Capital*, and Walter Oi, "Labor as a Quasi-Fixed Factor," *Journal of Political Economy*, December 1962.

period only if it has sound reason for expecting to recoup
later. Polarizing what obviously is a continuum, we can dis-
tinguish between general and specific training. At one end of
the continuum, perfectly general training will increase the
marginal productivity of the worker in other firms by as much
as in the firm providing the training. If workers are instant-
ly mobile in response to wage differentials, the firm providing
the training must offer its graduates the higher wages to which
their skills now entitle them, or else see them leave immediately for employment elsewhere. In a competitive labor market,
the mobile employee captures the benefits of general training.
Consequently, employers cannot be expected to finance it directly as a business activity. General training is mainly,
though certainly not exclusively, the province of the public
and private schools and universities. If general training is
not a joint product, employers will provide it only under highly circumscribed circumstances. The willingness of employees
to bear the cost is one such circumstance. Institutional factors such as the reserve clause in professional sports, which
converts general into specific training, is another. Low voluntary mobility rates may be the most important circumstance.
If the proportion of employees expected to be immobile is sufficiently large, employers can pay less than market wages to
generally trained workers and expect to recoup the training
cost of all their employees from the augmented productivity of
those who remain.
    At the other end of the continuum, perfectly specific
training raises the marginal productivity of a worker only in
the firm providing the training. The preparation of an astro-
naut, the familiarization of a secretary with the files and af-
fairs of her boss, and the rotation of a management trainee
through the various departments of the firm are all instances
of specific training. Who pays for specific training? Since
specific training does not raise the marginal productivity of a
worker elsewhere, it does not raise his opportunity wage. He
would be foolhardy to bear the full cost of such training. All
benefits evaporate if he is laid off or voluntarily finds it
advantageous to go elsewhere. Since alternative opportunities
have not been improved, there is no guarantee that he will be
rewarded for his enhanced skills if he stays with his current
employer. The employer must be expected to provide and to bear
the major cost of specific training. He earns his profit by
paying the employee a wage less than his productivity to the
firm but at least equal to his productivity elsewhere. High
employee turnover rates explain why an employer may be tempted
to pay a specifically trained worker a wage exceeding his opportunity marginal product. The employer earns a return on his
training investment only as long as the employee remains with
the firm. Since each departure of a trained worker forces the

employer to a new training expenditure, it is to his advantage
to attempt to reduce labor mobility. An obvious measure is to
share the benefits of enhanced productivity by offering the
trained worker a wage higher than could be earned elsewhere,
but still lower than his actual productivity. These higher
wages will reduce labor costs if they sufficiently curtail voluntary resignations. Jobs in which the employer pays the cost
of training and the employee gets some of the benefits are, of
course, highly attractive. Consequently, it may prove possible
to shift some of the costs of training back to the employee in
the form of lower wages during the training period.

The fact that training occurs in industry helps to explain
a number of important labor market phenomena. Apprentices, ac-
countants, lawyers, medical residents, and interns all receive
low starting wages considering their aptitudes and educational
background. This is because they are receiving and paying for
general training. The reduction of wages during the training
period, when workers pay a tuition, and the rise in wages after
graduation results in a positive correlation between income and
age. The earnings peak is reached quite young in activities in
which there is little or no training. Indeed, a flat age-
income profile is indicative of a job providing no learning opportunities. The more extensive the learning period, the later
in life the earnings peak.

The importance of training and hiring costs also explains
employer preferences for workers whose personal characteristics
suggest job stability. Teenagers and workers in their early
twenties tend to desire considerably shorter job tenure than do
older workers. Frequent job changes are an important mechanism
by which young workers explore both their own abilities and the
range of labor market opportunities. The fact that many younger persons do not have dependents and are free of major financial obligations facilitates the willingness to treat jobs as
exploratory experiences. Employers who bear the cost of the
learning experience quite naturally regard teenagers and other
single young persons lacking specialized skills as among the
least desirable of new employees. Many employers will hire
them only when older workers of comparable quality cannot be
found, except at higher wages. Likewise, many employers frown
on the clients of antipoverty agencies and retraining programs
because these clients have a reputation for job instability.
For a variety of reasons, women tend to earn lower wages than
men. Their shorter average labor force tenure is one of these
reasons. It reduces the profitability of both self-financed
and employer financed investment in training. The brunt of the
higher unemployment experienced during recessions is spread
quite unevenly throughout the labor force. As we shall see,

this differential incidence of cyclical unemployment is partially traceable to the reticence of employers to lay off workers in whose training they have an appreciable investment.

CONCLUSIONS

The work capability of any individual is the result of an interaction between his native capacities and the investments that have been made to further these capacities. Likewise, wages can be explained as the sum of the payments to raw labor and the return on investment in human capital. Expenditures on child-rearing, nutrition, health, education, training, job information, and mobility are all investments that raise the marginal productivity of labor. These investments are undertaken with different motivations by the individual, his parents, his employer, and society. For analytic purposes, the adult worker can be regarded as a produced factor, produced in a fashion somewhat analogous to a computer or a lathe.

Extensive statistical work indicates that the private rate of return on investment in education is robust, even after making a crude allowance for the fact that the inherently more able tend to acquire more education. White adult males do substantially better than women or nonwhites, and hence are more likely to invest in higher education. The abler benefit more than the less able, a fact that may reasonably limit the expansion in college attendance. Some dispute the social productivity of advanced general education, reasoning that the higher incomes of the educated are the result of employers using educational attainment as a screening device. The prevalent interpretation, though, is that general education does create human capital. If so, it is because education imparts the ability to learn rapidly and to cope with new problems in uncertain environments. Given the continued and massive increases in school attendance, the profitability of education will then depend crucially on a rapid rate of technical change.

4

The Functioning of the Labor Market

The static supply and demand schedules encountered in
elementary economics courses are invaluable guides to the expected direction of change in employment and wages. They are
the beginning, however, rather than the culmination of labor
market analysis. The labor market is typically in disequilibrium. It is a richly functioning organism subject to a never
ending sequence of external shocks. The economy is constantly
bombarded by technical change, taste shifts, reorderings of
social priorities, and cyclical fluctuations. By the very nature of things, the rate, direction of change, and skill bias
of these disturbances cannot be foreseen correctly by all labor
market participants.

Labor market decisions are made with an eye to the future
and are necessarily gambles. An expansion of employment in-
volving hiring and training costs is undertaken on the basis
of current high levels of demand. The expansion will prove
profitable only if the level of demand persists. Students decide to become engineers, lawyers, architects, economists, or
school teachers basing their decisions in part on recent levels
or rates of change in wages and employment. The correctness of
the decisions will depend, however, not on past history but on
future wage and employment trends. The training process for
these occupations is lengthy, and the market conditions that
made the occupational choice seem felicitous may have evaporated by graduation day. Ask the 1970 crop of new grammar school
and high school teachers, or physicists and engineers. Workers
make industrial and geographic choices, such as moving to California to take a job in the aerospace industry, or to Boston to
take a job in the electronics industry. These choices prove re-
warding only if favorable conditions persist in the aerospace
or electronics industry. All depends on the future, but the
future is unknowable. Even knowledge of the present is dis-
turbingly imperfect. The generation of information is expensive. The cost of obtaining complete knowledge is generally

greater than the marginal productivity of the knowledge to any single person or firm. Workers and employers rationally become reconciled to operating with incomplete information. The labor market is composed of uncertain actors, the wisdom of whose actions can be assessed only post hoc. Economists have come increasingly to the belief that the imperfections of knowledge and the heterogeneity of jobs and workers make the continuous gropings toward equilibrium best describable by probability or random processes. Our knowledge of these processes is admittedly quite limited. Therefore, in this chapter we will be able to discuss only some of the more salient features of the functioning of modern labor markets.

GROSS FLOWS AND WORKER MOBILITY

We will begin by investigating the interrelationship of labor market stocks and flows.[1] Stocks and flows can be differentiated by the existence of a time dimension. Flows have a time dimension. A flow can only be expressed per unit of time. The construction of new housing is a flow variable. To say that so many new houses are being constructed conveys no information. It is necessary to discuss the construction of new houses over some time horizon such as per day, per week, per month, per year, or per decade. In contrast, a stock, such as the housing inventory, does not have a time dimension. Rather, it must be measured at some moment of time.

In this chapter, we will be concerned with three major labor market stocks—employment, unemployment, and job vacancies. Each of these stocks is continually fed and relieved by a series of inflows and outflows. Employment is increased by hiring and reduced by quits, discharges, layoffs, and retirements. Unemployment is enhanced by quits, layoffs, and labor force entries, and reduced by new hires and labor force withdrawals. Vacancies are increased by the generation of new job openings and decreased by the filling of existing ones. These gross inflows and outflows are substantial. Each year between one and

---

[1]For a fuller discussion of these interrelationships, see Charles C. Holt and Martin H. David, "The Concept of Job Vacancies in a Dynamic Theory of the Labor Market," in *The Measurement and Interpretation of Job Vacancies* (New York: National Bureau of Economic Research, 1966). This chapter draws heavily on the Holt-David analysis, and on Holt's later work, particularly "Job Search, Phillip's Wage Relation, and Union Influence: Theory and Evidence," in *Microeconomic Foundations of Employment and Inflation Theory*, eds., Edmund S. Phelps, et al. (New York: W. W. Norton and Company, Inc., 1970).

two percent of the labor force leave the labor market because
of death, retirement, or family responsibilities. Two to three
percent enter the employment or unemployment stocks for the
first time. In addition, the massive back and forth movement
of housewives and youth between market and nonmarket activities
results in as many as three million persons entering and leaving the labor force each month. There is also an appreciable
amount of movement from employment to unemployment to employment, and from employment to employment. Median years on a
current job are only four. During 1961, 4.5 million persons
changed jobs voluntarily and another 3.5 million involuntarily.
Some of this mobility involves a willingness and an ability to
move across industrial, occupational, and geographic barriers.
Over half of the 11 million job shifts that occurred in 1961
involved movements of workers from one of 14 major industry
groups to another. Slightly less than half involved a shift
from one to another of the 22 major occupational groups.[2]

Job shifting frequently involves major geographic moves.
The Survey Research Center of the University of Michigan reports that 30 percent of all heads of families moved to a new
labor market area between 1950 and 1964, and that 65 percent of
all family heads were living in a different labor market area
than the one in which they were born.[3] Some impression of the
magnitude of the flows into and out of unemployment can be obtained by noting that 14.5 million different persons were unemployed in 1970, a year when the average monthly value for unemployment was only 4.1 million. Of these 14.5 million persons,
2.3 million experienced two and 2.5 million experienced three
or more nonconsecutive spells of unemployment.[4]

---

[2]Gertrude Bancroft and Stuart Garfinkle, "Job Mobility in
1961," U.S. Department of Labor, Bureau of Labor Statistics,
Monthly Labor Review, August, 1963, pp. 1-10. A study of gross
flows during 1949-53 testifies further to the ease with which
many workers move across industry lines. Of the manufacturing
workers unemployed in one month who found jobs in the next
month, one-third found jobs in some industry other than manufacturing. See David L. Kaplan, "Unemployment by Industry—
Some Comments on its Measurement and Behaviour," in *The Measurement and Behaviour of Unemployment* (Princeton, New Jersey: National Bureau of Economic Research, 1957), pp. 282-284.

[3]U.S. Department of Commerce, Area Redevelopment Administration,
*Economic Redevelopment Research: The Geographic Mobility of
Labor, Summary Report* (Washington, D.C.: U.S. Government Print-
ing Office, 1964).

[4]U.S. Department of Labor, Bureau of Labor Statistics, "Work
Experience of the Population in 1970," Special Labor Force Report Number 141, p. A-19.

Gross flows always loom large relative to changes in the size of stocks. There will be many job changes and a large number of persons obtaining jobs for the first time even during periods when the increase in employment is minimal. For that matter, many persons will be exiting from unemployment during periods when unemployment is increasing. If the number of employed or unemployed or of job vacancies remains unchanged from month to month, it is not because the same people are still employed or unemployed or the same jobs unfilled. Stability in the size of the stocks results from an exact balance of inflows and outflows rather than from unchanging membership. No net change in the stocks is always associated with an appreciable amount of gross change. The importance of this fact cannot be overemphasized. The size of the gross flows imparts an important element of flexibility to the system. It enables the economy to adjust rapidly to changes in the occupational, industrial, and geographic locus of demand for products and for workers.

THE IMMOBILE AND THE MOBILE WORKER

Many workers are reluctant to change jobs or employers. Many others are unlikely to be offered adequate inducement for change. Herbert S. Parnes estimated that in 1950, about a fifth of all workers had worked continuously during the preceding decade for one employer. A larger proportion, amounting to over a third, had served with only one employer though not necessarily continuously during the period.[5] In 1968, median years on a current job for men ages 45 to 54 was eleven.

Many workers are effectively insulated from the labor market by the structure of job rights and privileges. In a large number of establishments, promotion is from within and steps in the job hierarchy below supervisory level represent only minor and easily learned gradations in skill. Time on the job primarily differentiates those in the common labor pool from those with preferred semiskilled jobs. More generally, employers offer higher wages, longer vacations, more generous pensions, and first call on a large number of work place perquisites as rewards for employment longevity. It is not unusual for the office worker with the most seniority to have the most desirable space or office available to any employee of his grade. This preferred treatment is probably due to senior employees having more specific skills and being rewarded accord-

---

[5]*Research and Labor Mobility: An Appraisal of Research Findings in the United States* (New York: Social Science Research Council Bulletin No. 65, 1954), Chapter III.

ingly. In part, though, it may represent obeisance to the popularly held belief that perquisites should increase with age.
Higher wages for senior employees may have great merit as a recruiting aid and as a prop to morale, since they indicate automatic paths of progress to new workers. In any case, many
workers are receiving more from their current employer than
they could reasonably anticipate elsewhere. Given human iner-
tia, the satisfaction of informal social ties at the workplace
and in the community, and the various costs of moving, most
workers are not likely to change jobs unless they are offered
substantially more money than they are currently receiving.
Since they are likely to be offered less rather than more, most
workers are likely to stay put. They will not actively enter
the labor market unless there is a sharp relative improvement
in employment elsewhere or unless they are laid off.

The tendency to move and actual movement consequently are
heavily concentrated among certain labor force subgroups. Only
a modest fringe of workers appears to be highly responsive to
short-run variations in wages or job opportunities, but this
fringe is quite responsive. Its members shift jobs so rapidly
that the quit rate for production workers in manufacturing
firms normally averages over two percent a month.[6] The mobile
fringe consists largely of the young, recent hires, workers in
low wage industries, and the psychologically unfit. The mobile
young are either school attenders or out of school youth in
their late teens and early twenties. School attenders are primarily interested in part-time work during the school semester,
at Christmas, or summer vacation jobs. If they acquire jobs of
potentially more protracted duration, they eventually depart
because of school responsibilities, only to return after an interval to look for another job. For out of school youth, frequent job changing is an exploratory process in which abilities
are tested and the attractiveness of alternative environments
investigated. Job mobility is facilitated by the absence of
important financial obligations and by a spirit of restlessness.
The pressures imposed by age and marriage, of finding the right

---

[6]Turnover rates at some plants border on the unbelievable. A
recent study of a small midwest metal fabricating establishment
offering modest compensation and hard, dirty, and sometimes
dangerous work provides an example of how labor turnover com-
pels some firms to engage in continuous hiring activity. This
firm had hired 1670 workers over a period somewhat longer than
three years, but had a terminal employment level of only one
hundred and forty-three. See Edward D. Kalachek and John M.
Goering, eds., *Transportation and Central City Unemployment*
(St. Louis: Washington University Institute for Urban and Regional Studies, 1970), p. I-1.

niche or a reconciliation to not finding it, eventually dampen
this willingness to investigate. In 1961, the voluntary job
changing rate fell from 14 percent among males ages 18 to 24,
to two percent among males 45 to 64 years of age.[7]
New hires of whatever age have considerably higher quit
rates than other workers. Their job changing is a measure of
the paucity of information passed during the job interview.
Some of the more important attributes of the job and the worker
become apparent only after the two have been brought together.
The probationary period is a learning experience that frequently leads to a voluntary quit and a renewal of the job search.
Sometimes the quit is not entirely voluntary. Employers also
learn during the probationary period. Worker departure may be
a response to informal indications of the employer's disenchantment.
High quit rates are also associated with less desirable
jobs. A significant negative rank correlation between wage
rates and quit rates has been discerned.[8] Workers employed by
firms that reward seniority highly or that pay attractive wages
have relatively low quit rates. On the other hand, firms that
pay low wages, have unpleasant working conditions, or do not
substantially reward seniority have no strong basis for retain-
ing employee loyalty. They generally experience high quit
rates. Some of this turnover is an effort at self-improvement.
Some of it is simply lateral movement. It can be inferred that
many persons in low wage industries do not consider their wage
rates adequate incentive for working the standard 2,000 hour
work year. Since most jobs are full-time jobs, the desired
amount of leisure can be obtained only by quitting one job and
not seriously commencing search for another for some time. The
occupation of nurse's aide may be characterized by such a pattern of frequent job quitting and part-year retirement. In the
absence of promotion ladders or benefits geared to seniority,
nurse's aides suffer no capital loss from departing their present employer. A job at one hospital is basically as good as a
job at another hospital. Job quitters run little risk of permanent or long duration joblessness since other nurse's aides
will be taking leisure in the same fashion, assuring a steady
flow of new vacancies at other hospitals.
An appreciable number of workers will always be job hunting. Some will find it possible to scour the market effec-

---

[7]Gertrude Bancroft and Stuart Garfinkle, "Job Mobility in 1961,"
Monthly Labor Review, August 1963, p. 2.

[8]Lloyd Ulman, "Labor Mobility and the Industrial Wage Structure
in the Post-War United States," *Quarterly Journal of Economics*,
February 1965, p. 82.

tively and obtain a new job while still holding the old one.
In the recession year of 1961, approximately 40 percent of all
job changes took place without any intervening unemployment experience.[9] Job seeking by the employed is most prevalent in
professional and craft occupations in which lateral transfer is
frequent and workers are oriented more to the market than the
firm for their prosperity and security. For instance, while
still employed, college professors can go on lecture tours and
leisurely explore alternatives at other universities. The ma-
jority of job seekers, however, search from the less comfortable vantage point of unemployment. Some become unemployed
involuntarily when laid off or discharged. New labor market
entrants become unemployed as a matter of course when they initiate their job hunt. Others quit voluntarily, entering the
jobless state and generating a new vacancy at the same time.

Why should a worker ever quit a job before he has procured
himself a new one? By so doing he subjects himself to the certainty of some income loss, and to the possibility of serious
income loss if he has miscalculated his prospects. The effectiveness of informal antipirating agreements among personnel
managers, the difficulties of securing sufficient time off to
investigate job prospects adequately, and the need for leisure
in which to consider alternatives and make decisions are all
factors that explain why it is sometimes reasonable to quit one
job before initiating the search for another. Many workers
simply find it more efficient to search the market on a full-
time rather than on a part-time basis.[10] Of course, the fact
that workers are flesh and blood human beings should not be ig-
nored. All quits cannot be explained by the productivity of
specialization in search or as a necessary response to the
prevalence of antipirating agreements. Some workers quit their
jobs simply because they get temporarily fed up with work or
life. Many may not be too unhappy about casually perusing the
world between the cessation of one grind and the commencement
of another.

THE WORKER AND THE LABOR MARKET

The function of the labor market is to match a nonstandard
worker with a nonstandard job in a manner that satisfies the

---

[9]Gertrude Bancroft and Stuart Garfinkle, "Job Mobility in 1961,"
Monthly Labor Review, August 1963, p. 1.

[10]Armen A. Alchian, "Information Costs, Pricing and Resource
Unemployment," in *Microeconomic Foundations of Employment and
Inflation Theory*, eds., Edmund S. Phelps et al. (New York:
W. W. Norton and Company, Inc., 1970).

participants' requirements for wages, skill, and intangible relationships. Workers and vacancies are not easily matched.
The worker hunting for a vacancy and the job hunting for a
worker are both intricate, multidimensional entities. At his
current task, the worker is a bundle of productivity, ability
to cooperate with co-workers, learning capacity, promotability,
and stability on the job. The job is a bundle of current wages,
fringe benefits, promotion possibilities, pleasantness and interest or tedium of task and congeniality or unfriendliness of
colleagues and supervisors. For each worker there is an ideal
job. For each job there is an ideal worker. How are they to
meet? Even workers who have specialized skills will generally
have several thousand potential employers. The modestly
skilled worker may have several hundred thousand potential employers.

The adage about ideal marriages being made in heaven could
pertain to matching jobs to workers. Only the omniscience of
the deity could ensure ideal job-worker matches throughout the
system. Workers and employers are not omniscient. They start
out with limited information and they obtain more only at a
cost. An ideal match in a world in which information costs are
zero may no longer be ideal when information costs are positive.
In hunting for a higher paying or more challenging job, the
worker must bear in mind the psychic and money costs of job applications and the loss of income while unemployed. In determining how long to hunt for workers who will labor for lower
wages or workers who have greater skill, the employer must consider the costs of interviewing and the costs of losing production because jobs remain unfilled during the search. How long
should the search be conducted? The decision rule for search-
ers is straightforward enough. Continue searching so long as
the expected discounted benefits of the search exceed the expected discounted costs. The problem in the real world is that
workers hunting for jobs and employers hunting for workers are
not sure about the benefits of additional search. At best,
they can form probabilistic judgments—there is a ten percent
chance per period of time that a worker or an offer with specified characteristics will develop.

Worker Adjustments

The demand schedule for a relatively standardized commodity is expressible in price and quantity terms. For instance,
10 million ties might be sold annually at an average price of
$5, 12 million ties at an average price of $4.50, and 13 million ties at an average price of $4.00. This form of expres-
sion is not appropriate for an individual who has only one item
—his services—to sell, and who will either consummate a

transaction or not. Nonetheless, workers can usefully think of
demand schedules for their services. They are aware from casual observation that wages and working conditions vary from firm
to firm. Their services are worth more to some employers than
to others. They are eligible for a large number of jobs, some
of which are clearly preferable to others. The preferable jobs
may not be available or discovered immediately. It takes time
to discover which are the desirable employers and which of
these are actively hiring. Only a limited number of job applications and interviews can be fitted into any finite time period. Some of these interviews will not result in offers; others
will result in low wage offers. The appropriate demand schedule for the individual is then a random one, stipulating the
probability per unit of time of being hired as a function of
the wage rate. There is a one percent chance per week that he
will be offered a job paying $5 an hour or more, a five percent
chance of an offer of $4 or more, a 20 percent chance of an of-
fer of $2 or more, and so on. The worker who is aware of the
demand schedule for his services is aware simply of this probability distribution of offers.

The *neoclassical theory of job search* assumes the worker's awareness of the demand schedule.[11] There should normally be a wage sufficiently low that the typical worker
would be certain of being offered a job paying at least that
much during any week of reasonably intense job search. There
is thus a voluntary or desired aspect to search unemployment.
A worker can obtain employment promptly simply by setting a
sufficiently low acceptance wage. However, the rational worker
will not seek to minimize unemployment and maximize days working. He will willingly bear unemployment if the expected discounted gains of the job search exceed its expected discounted
cost. Neither will this worker seek to maximize his wage rate.
The highest attainable wage will normally have a low probability of offer associated with it. It would make little sense
for a middle-aged man to turn down a $4 an hour offer to go
hunting for a $5 an hour job which might be found only after
several additional years of search. The rational worker will
weigh the benefits of a higher wage against the costs of search.
He will set an acceptance wage accordingly and hunt until he
finds a suitable offer. The unemployment experienced during
this hunt is part of the cost of searching alternatives adequately. It is not a waste but an investment. Of course, the

---

[11]This theory is most fully developed by Donald F. Gordon and
Allan Hynes, "On the Theory of Price Dynamics," in *Microeco-
nomic Foundations of Employment and Inflation Theory*," eds.,
Edmund S. Phelps et al. (New York: W. W. Norton and Company,
Inc., 1970), pp. 369-393.

acceptance wage need not be rigid over time if liquidity is
limited. Pressing financial need may lead to its gradual ero-
sion. Measures to provide additional liquidity, such as improved unemployment compensation and severance benefits, will
then actually result in longer job searches and higher unemployment rates.

Gordon and Hynes observe that the worker who has labor
services to sell is in a similar position to the apartment
owner who has a vacancy. Workers and apartments are both heterogeneous bundles of attributes. Consider the decision making
problems and processes of the apartment owner. Given the current organization of the real estate market, apartments can be
appraised adequately only by direct inspection. They can be
shown only to a limited number of viewers during any time period. A large proportion of these viewers might be interested
in renting the apartment at the right price, but the right
price varies sharply from viewer to viewer. Assume that the
apartment owner knows the probability per unit of time of renting his apartment, which is associated with any rent. If the
owner's sole concern is to keep his apartment occupied, he will
reduce the asking rent to such a low level that one of the
viewers is sure to rent on the first day. Such behavior would
obviously be eccentric. A sensible owner is interested in
maximizing the present value of net rents received, and not
the number of days that the apartment is occupied. He should
set a rent that achieves this objective, given the probability
function. The apartment should then be held vacant at this
rent until an occupant is found.

The neoclassical theory of an income or utility maximizing
workers' searching a known probability distribution of offers
is a parable. As such it is useful, revealing both the necessity for probabilistic decision making and the beneficent nature of much unemployment. Still it is not a description of
reality. It abstracts from the real world problems of ephem-
eral options. For many workers, a thorough investigation of
the job market will be inhibited by the terrible fragility of
offers. The worker may desire to keep an option on one good
offer while continuing to hunt for yet a better one. Most frequently, though, he is forced to a quick "yes" or "no" answer.
This theory also abstracts from the problem of incomplete information. Some workers do have a fairly good impression of
the parameters of the demand schedule for their services. Examples would include the professional and the artisan whose
normal work activities involve contact with employers other
than his own, and the graduating college student who benefits
from a well-organized formal placement service. It seems unlikely, though, that the typical worker with some years of job
tenure, isolated as he is from the labor market, would have
such knowledge. The knowledge obtained from earlier job hunts

may be of little value since rapid technical change, income
growth, and the vagaries of public and private tastes are continuously rearranging the structure of the demand for labor.
Many workers would have to reconnoiter the market first and
sample the probability distribution of offers to acquire an impression of the demand for their services. Only then could
they set an acceptance wage that would maximize their expected
net discounted income flow.

This reconnoitering will not always be a painless process.
The middle-aged worker with lengthy job tenure and a fund of
specific skills is likely to suffer a substantial capital loss
if he is laid off. The value of his skills has eroded. He
will earn less in the future than he did in the past. Considerable market probing may be required before he discovers and
adjusts to his new range of alternatives. Much time may pass
before some people can bring themselves to accept facts that
they prefer not to accept. Search unemployment is voluntary.
At the same time, exposure to unemployment may be a powerful
disciplinary force leading to a readjustment of worker aspirations and behavior.

Is the typical worker likely to scan the market or make
decisions in the calculating and rational fashion described
above? The empirical literature on job hunting portrays a less
purposeful economic actor. The typical search is described as
fumbling and disorganized. According to a classic and representative source, "Workers have only fragmentary information
about other job openings, rates of pay or earnings, and other
conditions of employment beyond the jobs they have held. . . .
Perhaps they do not usually weigh alternatives and choose the
job with the greatest net economic advantage."[12]

Consequently, it is worthwhile examining the *aspiration
level hypothesis*, an alternative model of worker behavior
first suggested by Professor Charles Holt. He hypothesized
that the acceptance wage is determined by initial market percep-
tions and internal aspirations and is modified by the job hunt
experience. As the theory is developed by William Barnes, the
relationship between the wage on the last job and the acceptance wage for the new job depends on the extent to which unemployment is regarded as a sign of personal failure, the intensity with which failure is feared, and the wage received on the
last job relative to group norms.[13] Initially, the voluntary
quit will be thinking of a better paying job; the layoff per-

---

[12]Charles A. Myers and George P. Schultz, *The Dynamics of the
Labor Market* (New York: Prentice-Hall, 1951), pp. 46-47 and 72.

[13]William Barnes, "Wage Flexibility of Unemployed Jobseekers"
(Ph.D. thesis, Washington University, 1970), Chapter 3.

haps of an equivalently well-paying one. If a job offer equal
or superior to expectations is encountered, it will be accepted.
Otherwise, the search will continue. If it continues for sufficiently long, the disappointment of expectations and the evapo-
ration of savings will eventually result in a downward revision
of aspirations. The reservation wage for full-time work for
many employed male workers with dependents undoubtedly lies considerably below their actual earnings. Such workers have substantial family obligations and lack attractive or productive
nonmarket alternatives. Unemployed and faced with the prospect
of protracted joblessness, they are under pressure to behave in
a manner that will increase the probability of finding a job.

Unemployment is a learning experience. A lengthy unemployment duration indicates that initial aspirations were unrealistic. The longer one is unemployed, the lower the wage one is
willing to accept. In a good labor market in which jobs are
readily available, unemployed workers, quits in particular, may
achieve higher wages on their new jobs than they received on
their old jobs. In a labor market in which jobs are scarce,
the reverse is likely.

Empirical Evidence

As noted earlier, there is a solid body of empirical
evidence on the occupational, industrial, and geographical
adaptability of unemployed workers. Further, those unemployed
workers who face bleak labor market prospects do show some
willingness to accept lower wages. To cite two plant shutdown
studies, Adams and Aronson found that the average starting wage
at their new job for 141 International Harvester workers displaced in 1950 was 45 to 50 cents an hour less than previous
earnings.[14] Miernyk reported that 64 percent of the workers
displaced by a textile plant closing, who found new employment,
received lower weekly earnings.[15]

A comparison of the neoclassical and the aspiration level
theory of job search gives rise to an interesting and important
question. Is this willingness to accept lower wages and make
other adjustments an immediate or a gradual response to a
changed demand situation? Does the typical worker scan the

---

[14]Leonard P. Adams and Robert L. Aronson, *Workers and Industrial Change; A Case Study of Labor Mobility* (Ithaca, New York:
Cornell University Press, 1957).

[15]William H. Miernyk, *Inter-Industry Labor Mobility; The Case
of the Displaced Textile Worker* (Boston: Northeastern University Press, 1955).

market upon disemployment, decide on an acceptance wage, and,
liquidity sufficing, search until that wage is secured? If the
optimum course of behavior is to accept a wage lower than that
earned previously, is the fact realized immediately or after a
brief reconnoiter of the market? Alternatively, does the willingness to adjust increase substantially in response to the
length of the job search? The evidence is mixed. The two most
comprehensive econometric studies in this area suggest that
workers who perceive the necessity for downward adjustments
perceive it quite early in their unemployment experience.

Barnes used multivariate techniques to analyze a sample of
2500 unemployed workers registered with public employment services in 12 cities in 1962.[16] These workers had, on the average,
been unemployed for five and a half months and stated that they
were willing to accept wages 14 percent below their prior earnings. Barnes's findings are quite interesting. He reports
that the decline in the acceptance wage was 5.8 percentage
points more for layoffs than for quits. Workers perceiving
their unemployment experience as due to personal deficiencies
showed wage declines 3.2 percentage points greater than those
who perceived unemployment as a chance experience caused by a
shortage of jobs. Poor expectations of future employment increased wage declines by 7.7 percentage points more than good
expectations. The acceptance wage declined 10 percentage
points for each dollar of the prior wage. However, it declined
by only two-tenths of a percentage point for each month of unemployment. Similarly, in a study of a 1961 sample of 3,000
Minnesota workers with an average unemployment duration of
7.5 months, Hirschel Kasper found a decline of only about .4
percent per month.[17] On the other hand, studies of relatively
skilled workers affected by layoffs at Boeing and Martin suggest that asking wages fell at the much more pronounced monthly
rates of 2.6 and 1.4 percent respectively.[18] The Kasper (and
implicitly the Barnes) study has been criticized by Arnold Katz
for using single equation estimating techniques. Katz reasons
that the length of unemployment affects the acceptance wage,
but that the acceptance wage also affects the length of unemployment. Consequently, simultaneous equation estimating techniques are most appropriate. Utilizing such techniques, he
finds that on entering the unemployment stock, the typical

---

[16]"Wage Flexibility of Unemployed Job Seekers," pp. 58-87.

[17]"The Asking Price of Labor and the Duration of Unemployment,"
Review of Economics and Statistics, May 1967.

[18]United States Arms Control and Disarmament Agency, *The Dyna-
Soar Control Cancellation* (Washington, D.C.: U.S. Government
Printing Office, 1965).

worker aspires to a wage substantially above his prior earning.
Each month of unemployment then results in a decline of approximately eight percent in his acceptance wage.[19]

Information and Search Cost

A substantial amount of unemployment occurs because workers quite reasonably do not take the first job available but
instead search for the optimum, or at least for a reasonably
good offer. Search is time-consuming because of limitations on
the amount of information a person can obtain during any time
period. These limitations are an appropriate area for public
policy concern. A visionary might contemplate a labor market
serviced by an elaborate computer network. Each evening the
computers would be fed information on all the pertinent and
quantifiable aspects of job hunters and job vacancies. Each
morning workers would receive a rank ordering of jobs that met
their requirements and for which they were qualified. Employers would receive a rank ordering of workers who had the appropriate skills and backgrounds and were willing to accept the
company's wages and working conditions. Such a scheme would
greatly improve the flow of information to labor market participants. Required search time and the duration of unemployment
would be reduced. Indeed, workers could inform the computer
service of their availability several days before their intend-
ed quit or layoff became effective. They would have some opportunity while still employed to scan available opportunities.
Unless they expected the market for their services to improve
decidedly in the near future, or unless they required substantial leisure for decision making, they could possibly move
promptly from job to job without any intervening unemployment
experience.

The United States Employment Service (USES) is slowly
evolving in the direction of a computerized information dissem-
inating network, but so far its market penetration is modest.
It accounts for only a small portion of job-worker matches.
The USES suffers from a simultaneity problem. Its ties to unemployment compensation offices (now being shorn) and its social obligation to place minority group members and marginal
workers have jaundiced its reputation among both workers and
employers. Good workers avoid the USES because it does not receive the best job listings. Good employers avoid the USES because it cannot deliver the better workers. The likelihood
that improved information flows would substantially reduce

---

[19]"Acceptance Wages and the Length of Unemployment" (Mimeo.,
University of Pittsburgh, 1972).

search unemployment is sufficiently alluring to place some premium on efforts to upgrade and expand job placement services.
Still, penetration possibilities would probably remain modest,
even if the image problem of the USES were solved. Central
placement bureaus would have to become substantially more sophisticated before desirable employers permitted them to pre-
screen applicants, and they would have to develop considerably
more information about the informal aspects of jobs before good
workers were willing to rely heavily on them.

A glance at job search behavior is revealing. Workers can
conduct their job searches through formal channels such as public and private employment agencies and newspaper "help wanted"
ads, or through informal channels relying on information obtained from friends and relatives and applications at the plant
gate. Formal channels permit an extensive market search and
provide a wide view of available job opportunities. However,
they account for less than a fourth of all placements. Job
hunters rely primarily on informal search techniques, even
though these techniques narrowly restrict the view of available
opportunities. The prime importance of information provided by
friends and relatives and gate applications is cited in study
after study. This is understandable since the informal search
techniques personalize the initial contact with the employer,
and at times provide authenticated information on conditions of
work. How fast is the work pace? What are the opportunities
for promotion? How easygoing or how demanding are the supervisors? A friend or relative in the plant or office is the best
possible source for such information. An employment counselor
conceivably might obtain the same information, but his views
are unlikely to be treated with the same degree of respect and
trust.

Albert Rees aptly compares the position of the job hunter
(and the employer) with that of the prospective used car pur-
chaser.[20] It is more important to obtain a bit of additional
information about the quality of a used car or a job that might
fall into the satisfactory category than it is to hunt for additional price quotations. In the used car market as in the
employment market, the value attached to information depends on
its source. Thus, one might be willing to pay more for a car
previously owned by a friend or a relative who will vouch for
its conditions and whose driving habits are known, than one
would pay to a stranger.

Finally, the importance of labor market information should
not be exaggerated. Obvious examples come to mind of instances
when information is hard to come by and an organized employment

---

[20]Albert Rees, "Information Networks in Labor Markets," *American Economic Review*, May 1966, pp. 559-566.

exchange is invaluable. If the aerospace industry closes down
on the West Coast, stranding a large number of engineers, there
is need for a placement service offering information on jobs
elsewhere in the country. Likewise, information about jobs in
other areas and mobility assistance can really matter for workers in small isolated towns where the major employer has just
closed his plant. Teenagers leaving school may not know much
about the adult labor market or how to canvass it. There certainly are many disoriented people who would benefit greatly
from a few hours or a few days with a competent employment
counselor. In other instances, however, the improved flow of
job information might be only modestly valuable.

　　After all, most Americans have nonexotic skills, live in
large metropolitan areas, have cars, are friendly with people
who do the same type of work they do, and are capable of reading want ads. Under full employment circumstances, an industrial worker, a salesman, a secretary, or a janitor living in
a major metropolitan area should be able on his own to canvass
a significant number of job opportunities in a week. In many
instances, the duration of unemployment results from a wait
rather than from a search. All types of jobs are not continuously available. An unemployed worker may recognize that his
best pay and promotion prospects are with an electronics firm.
Electronics firms are not hiring now but may be later in the
month. The worker may find it advantageous to wait for that
prospect rather than to accept some other job immediately or
to search prospects that he considers inferior.

THE EMPLOYER AND THE LABOR MARKET

　　We assume that employers are profit maximizers. The firm
desires a work force of a size that will enable it to conduct
its operations in the most profitable fashion. To obtain such
a work force, the employer will hire and retain workers only
if they contribute at least as much to his revenues as to his
costs. This decision rule leads to an inversely sloped demand
schedule for labor. The firm will hire fewer workers at high
wages than at low wages. This is due in part to an output effect. Higher wages lead to higher marginal costs. In turn,
they result in higher product prices and a lower unit level of
sales. In part, the negative slope of the labor demand schedule is due to a substitution effect. Our technological knowledge is sufficiently rich that output can be produced in a
variety of fashions. The firm can use production techniques
ranging from labor intensive to capital intensive. To take a
homely example, grass can be cut with much labor and a scissors;
it can also be cut with less labor and a hand mower, or with
progressively less labor and more capital congealed into progressively larger power mowers. Employers can choose between

these alternative production techniques on the basis of their
cost. They select that capital-labor combination that is least
costly for the expected level of output. As wages increase, it
becomes profitable to select increasingly capital intensive
techniques.

The demand schedule for labor slopes downward because at
higher wages less output will be sold and because at any output
level less labor will be used in the production process. The
workings of this inverse relationship frequently take considerable time. Hence, the relationship is not always easily dis-
cernible. The demand for labor may be relatively inelastic in
the short-run, but it becomes increasingly elastic as time proceeds. Consumer lethargy and the fixity of capital are responsible for the short-run inelasticity of demand. Since higher
wages normally lead to higher product prices, consumers can be
expected to respond by reducing unit purchases. However, given
the importance of habit and of complementarities in consumption
patterns, consumer response will not be instantaneous. Likewise, the firm having constructed plant and equipment has irre-
trievably committed itself to one form of capital until its
facilities become economical to replace. It has given hostages
to the future, and will suffer if wages rise above the rates at
which its capital-labor ratio is predicated.

With a given configuration of equipment, substitution possibilities may well be minimal. In some cases, the design of
equipment enforces relatively rigid capital-labor coefficients.
The facility cannot be safely operated without a specified con-
tingent of labor, while additional workers make no contribution
whatsoever to output. In such an instance, employment will be
invariant with respect to the wage rate so long as the wage
rate is sufficiently low to make operation of the facility at
all worthwhile. To cite an example from the past, a ten-story
office building with manually operated elevators is not likely
to discharge any of its operators, even in response to a very
large wage increase. Higher wages will, however, hasten the
economic obsolescence of the manually operated elevators and
speed their replacement by automatically operated elevators.

In addition to wage rates, the size of the firm's desired
work force depends on the number of workers currently employed
(they are cheaper than new workers since training and hiring
expenses are already water over the dam), expected future sales,
order backlogs, inventory size, and productivity.[21] If the
actual work force diverges in size from the desired work force,
the firm will be spurred to corrective action. If the actual
work force exceeds the desired work force, hiring should cease,
while some combination of quits, retirements, and layoffs is

---

[21]The treatment here closely follows the articles by Holt cited
in footnote 1 of this chapter.

allowed to curtail the work force. If the desired work force
is greater than the actual work force, vacancies will exist and
the firm will seek to expand. A vacancy exists whenever the
firm is willing at going wage rates to hire more workers of the
same quality as its current staff. Deviations of the actual
from the desired work force are not the only cause of job vacancies. The components of the vacancy stock can be defined as
follows:

$$V = (E^* - E) + (\hat{q} + \hat{r})T + (E^*)T \qquad (1)$$

where V = vacancies
      E = employment
      q = quits
      r = retirements
      T = average lead time for hiring and training workers
      $*$ = desired quantities
      $\wedge$ = anticipated quantities

All vacancies are not of equal moment. The last two terms
on the right-hand side of equation (1) represent prudent pre-
cautions rather than current shortages. The firm does not need
the productive services of these workers today. It is bidding
for labor because it will need trained replacements for future
separations and for anticipated growth. These anticipatory vacancies are a sign of good personnel management. They are not
a measure of labor market disequilibrium. Their coexistence
with unemployment is not a sign of structural imbalance. The
current labor deficit is measured only by the first component
on the right-hand side of equation (1). The firm would be operating most profitably if it currently had $(E^* - E)$ additional
workers of the quality normally hired, provided they were ob-
tainable at going wage rates.

The Supply of Labor to the Firm

The ability of the firm to hire these workers depends on
the slope of its supply curve of labor, a subject to which we
now turn. Whatever the shape of the aggregate supply schedule
of labor, the supply schedule of the firm will not be backward
bending. Part of the leisure purchased by higher wages is obtained through a readjustment of the burden of home chores and
involves reductions in market work by other members of the family. This interfamily reallocation of effort has no relevance
for the supply schedule of the firm unless all family members
are among its actual or reasonably potential employees. Higher
wages may well result in a reduction in market input by current
employees, but this should be more than compensated for by the
attraction of additional workers from other firms.

Some firms will have the perfectly elastic supply schedule
that characterizes perfect competitors in the labor market.
Other firms, called *monopsonists*, will have monopoly power on
the buying side. They will face a positively sloped supply
schedule, and will be able to expand employment only by paying
higher wages and considerably higher labor costs. Consider a
firm employing 200 workers and paying $2.00 an hour. Its hour-
ly wage bill is $400. Suppose the firm wishes to expand to 220
workers, but can do so only if it offers an hourly wage of
$2.10. If its current employees must also be paid this rate,
the hourly wage bill rises to $462. Hiring 20 additional work-
ers has increased the hourly wage bill by $62. The 20 new
workers are paid an hourly wage of $2.10 but their marginal
cost is $3.10 per hour.

The position of the perfect competitor in the labor market
and of the monopsonist can be compared graphically in Figure 1.
Case A is that of the perfect competitor. As demand increases,
he expands employment from Q_1 to Q_2, continuing to pay the wage
P_1. Case B is that of the monopsonist. His increase in demand
is confronted by a positively sloped supply curve. Optimizing
behavior calls for an increase in wages to P_2. This results in
a marginal cost of labor of P_3, and an expansion in employment
smaller than that of the perfect competitor.

A firm's labor market position can alter easily. It may
be a monopsonist at one moment and a perfect competitor or wage
taker at another. The major influences on the slope of its
supply schedule can be summarized into four factors: (1) the
aggregate labor supply-demand balance; (2) the needs of the
firm relative to the size of the local labor market; (3) the
psychic benefits offered to its employees; and (4) the time period under consideration.

During periods of high unemployment, most firms should be
able to attract additional workers at the going wage rate regardless of the magnitude of their labor needs. As an extreme
instance, higher wage offers were not necessary for recruiting
additional labor during the depression of the 1930s. Firms
seeking to expand employment during recessions can draw on
their previously laid-off workers who are awaiting recall, on
workers who were laid off by other firms and who do not anticipate immediate recall, and on new labor market entrants.
Things become different if the labor market tightens, especially if full employment is reached or if excess demand arises.
More of the firms seeking to expand employment find that the
only way to meet their labor needs is to raise wages and bid
workers away from their present jobs. However, given the large
amount of labor turnover that occurs and the year-to-year increases in the size of the labor force, many firms will find
the relevant range of their supply schedule to be perfectly
elastic even under full employment circumstances.

Case A

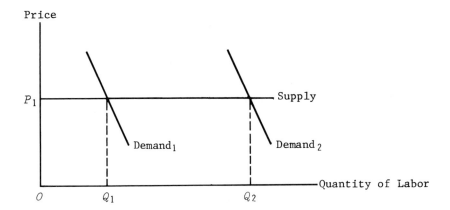

Case B

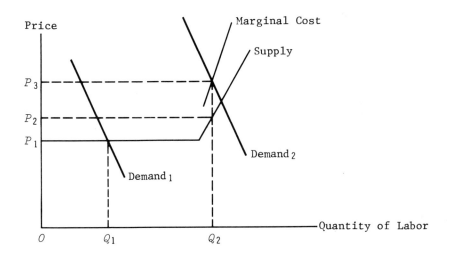

Figure 1.   Supply of Labor to the Firm

     The small firm employing unspecialized labor and situated
in a major urban labor market is likely to find that it can attract additional labor at the going wage rate from the ranks of
new entrants and from among those dissatisfied with their current jobs. The bigger the firm is relative to the size of the
market, the more likely it is to be a monopsonist. It should
be noted that the 500 largest corporations (ranked by sales)
had 14 million employees in 1970, and the federal government,
including Armed Forces, had six million employees. The big
firm located in a small town and accounting for most of the
town's employment is the textbook example of a monopsonist.
It may already be employing most of the local people whose talents or inclinations suit them to its operations. If it wishes
to hire additional labor, it may have to recruit outside the
community. Higher wages may then be necessary to induce workers to shift residences or to undertake long-distance commuting.
     If all jobs offered the same net psychic benefits, workers
would choose between jobs purely on the basis of wage rates.
If all jobs paid the same wage rates also, workers would choose
employers by flipping a coin. Once workers become employed,
they might develop attachments toward their particular job,
since many people have a strong affinity for familiar neighbor-
hoods and workplaces. Nonetheless, new labor market entrants
and natural labor turnover would generally suffice to ensure a
perfectly elastic supply schedule for all firms at the going
wage rate. All jobs, however, do not offer the same bundle of
psychic advantages and disadvantages. Some jobs afford opportunities for intellectual creativity or for the exercise of
power or the display of craftsmanship. Less happily, some jobs
are conducive to nervous strain or physical fatigue or boredom.
To complicate matters further, workers have different taste
buds and rank psychic benefits differently. A job that would
yield great satisfactions for one person could generate great
frustrations for another.
     In the fullest and most correct statement of the theory of
occupational choice, workers are regarded as maximizing not the
discounted lifetime stream of earnings but rather that stream
plus net psychic benefits. Opportunities then exist for trade-
offs between income and the pleasantness of the job. In seeking to obtain maximum net advantages from employment, workers
will sometimes take lower paying jobs that offer more job satisfaction. At other times, wages will be sufficiently high to
bribe them into less satisfying jobs. The occupational mix of
jobs and the pleasures associated with the production process
differ from firm to firm. The implications are obvious.
Small firms may be able to hire workers so enamored of their
particular bundle of psychic benefits that they are willing to
accept lower wages than they might earn elsewhere. If the firm
seeks to expand, it may eventually have to appeal to workers

indifferent to choosing between its psychic benefits and to
those offered elsewhere. Further expansion could require recourse to workers who must be paid a premium to overcome their
distaste for the activity.

When university enrollments and the need for faculty were
much smaller than they are currently, college administrators
were in the happy position of being able to hire professors who
so enjoyed teaching that they were willing to accept low wages.
As the desired size of college faculties rose, administrators
increasingly had to recruit from a population that regarded
government and industry as attractive alternatives to teaching.
Increasingly higher wages were needed to attract people with
these taste patterns into university life. As a general rule,
firms of substantial size will face a perfectly elastic supply
schedule if their community contains an appreciable number of
qualified persons who possess the same set of preferences.
They will face an upward sloping schedule if preferences vary
significantly among workers. We actually know very little
about the importance and sensitivity of taste factors. Income
aside, are most Detroit clerical workers indifferent to selecting between working for General Motors or for the Bank of Detroit? Are most Birmingham production workers indifferent to
selecting between steel production and metal fabrication? Does
the typical factory worker care whether he is employed in the
rubber industry, electrical machinery production, or in assem-
bling airplanes?

Time is the most important determinant of the elasticity
of supply. The longer the time span under consideration, the
higher will be the elasticity of supply. Given enough time,
information about job availability and wage rates becomes widely disseminated. The capacity of educational and training facilities grows to match demand. Recruiting is concentrated
among new entrants who are not tied to other employers by seniority or community attachment. In the long run, all supply
schedules would become perfectly elastic if it were not for differences in taste. On the other hand, if we consider a period
of time so brief that recruiting is impossible, the supply
schedule of labor to the firm will be perfectly inelastic.
More to the point, firms attempting to expand employment substantially over a period of weeks may find that they have to
pay higher wages. The larger and the more urgent the hiring
needs of the firm, the more its options will be confined to
those workers already probing the job market. Firms seeking to
hire substantial numbers of workers rapidly become dynamic monopsonists.

Employer Adjustments

Most large companies find it desirable from time to time
to engage in large scale and rapid work force expansion. Their
expansion needs most frequently occur when employment is high
elsewhere, and good workers hard to come by. Some economists
argue that wage increases are an ineffective tool for coping
with such urgent recruiting needs.[22] Information about wage
rate increases disseminates through the labor market too slowly.
Companies need some surer technique for recruiting rapidly.
One long run strategy followed by some large firms in noncom-
petitive industries is to pay a regular wage higher than the
short run market clearing wage and to earn a reputation as a
good employer. This strategy will result in a day-to-day flow
of applicants exceeding the company's needs. This steady flow
is a form of excess capacity which the company taps whenever it
wishes to expand employment rapidly. The persistent payment of
premium wages seems an expensive way to advertise for workers.
However, the reputation of being a high wage payer permits the
firm to follow a selective hiring policy. High wages may be a
good bargain if they normally allow the firm to hire exception-
ally able workers and to meet rapid expansion needs simply by
moving somewhat farther down the queue of applicants.
Only a limited number of firms can pursue this strategy.
Most monopsonists must find some other means for coping with
the high marginal cost of labor. The monopsonist would like a
technique for segregating markets, so that he could pay new
workers the premiums required for their recruitment without
having to raise wages for current employees. However, if the
new and old workers are indistinguishable, it will generally
be advisable to pay both groups the same wage. Few things are
richer sources of discontent, low productivity, and high quit
rates than the practice of paying workers performing the same
work in the same establishment different wages. Paying the
same wages to workers of different productive efficiency may
prove to be a less dangerous method of discrimination. An upward sloping supply schedule for workers of a given quality may
induce employers to lower hiring standards. Lower quality
workers would normally be earning less than the firm's going
wage rate. Consequently, they should be available in indefinite numbers.
Lowering hiring standards involves a rise in labor costs,
but one that is restricted to the newly hired workers and may
be less onerous to the employer than the alternative of an
across-the-board wage increase. The expenses involved in

---

[22]See Alfred Kuhn, "Market Structure and Wage-Push Inflation,"
Industrial and Labor Relations Review, January 1959.

lowering hiring standards become evident once they are recognized as a proxy for nonwage costs. A firm that maintains high hiring standards is more likely: (1) to incur only relatively modest training expenditures to bring a worker to an acceptable level of productivity; (2) to obtain workers who will perform satisfactorily, thus saving the expenses incurred when a recruitment error is made, only to be terminated by a discharge; (3) to safeguard itself against the expense of hiring workers who have a high propensity either to quit or to cause disciplinary problems.

To recapitulate, vacancies arising from an excess of desired over actual employment are normally traceable to an increase in the expected sales of the firm (although they could also result from an inability to replace departing employees). The employer will be able to satisfy his recruiting needs by accepting a higher proportion of gate applicants if his short-run supply schedule of labor is perfectly elastic. Otherwise, vacancies will persist. The number of applicants of requisite quality will not be sufficient to satisfy the firm's expansion plans. Profits would be higher if only production could be increased. The increasing number or lengthening duration of vacancies means the firm must resort to overtime or else lose potential sales or allow inventories to slip below optimum levels. These are all expensive expedients. The persistence of vacancies signals the firm that it must undertake measures to augment its hiring ability. These measures will be costly. They will be undertaken only because the alternative—operating with a work force of less than desired size—is even more costly. The firm can improve its hiring ability by increasing expenditures on help wanted ads or private employment agencies and other recruiting aids, by raising wages, or by lowering hiring standards. We will concentrate on the latter two measures since they are the adjustments of greatest importance.

The firm's recruiting ability depends on the wages it offers and on the hiring standards it sets. There should be a number of combinations of wages and hiring standards capable of yielding the same improvement in recruiting ability. A firm that raises wages sufficiently will make its jobs so attractive that it can expand without lowering hiring standards. A firm that lowers hiring standards sufficiently can tap a large enough reservoir of potential workers so that it can expand without raising wages.[23]

---

[23]In some instances, the general educational prerequisites or responsibility requirements of the job are so rigid that they preclude the option of lowering hiring standards. This would be the case when the costs of materials or machinery is great and when workers could seriously damage the materials or

Since the firm is a profit maximizer, it will not automatically embrace either such strategy. Rather, it will seek to expand employment by choosing the combination of changes that minimizes outlays. The firm seeking to hire new employees at a rapid rate is likely to find that it is cost minimizing to proceed by both raising wages and lowering hiring standards.[24]

The social implications of this analysis are important. Dynamic monopsony and the motivation for rapid hiring are most likely to appear when the system is near, at, or beyond full employment. Consequently, hiring standards should be high when unemployment is high and low when unemployment is low. Workers with bad work records, low aptitudes for productive endeavor, or characteristics that employers dislike may easily be frozen out of job opportunities when unemployment and hiring standards are high. They are likely to find jobs most readily when unemployment and hiring standards are low. Furthermore, they are most likely to progress up the occupational ladder into higher paying and more satisfying jobs. Lawrence Slifman estimates that a one percentage point decline in the unemployment rate is associated with 525,000 more disadvantaged workers moving into more favored occupations.[25]

Hiring Standards

Hiring standards are sufficiently important to merit further analysis. If wages were specific to the individual, if the production process involved little cooperation, and if there were no expensive equipment susceptible to damage, employers would not impose hiring standards. Take the case of harvest workers engaged in hand picking and paid on a straight piece-rate basis.[26] Employers show no concern over the characteristics of these workers, simply hiring whoever appears. However, the harvest labor market, far from being representa-

---

[23]cont. the machinery if they were of inadequate skill or responsibility. (Examples would be a diamond cutter or a cyclotron operator.) The firm seeking to expand employment is then restricted to the higher wage rate route. In most instances, though, hiring standards are flexible.

[24]For the analytic derivation of this conclusion, see Lawrence Slifman, "Occupational Mobility of Low Income Workers" (Ph.D. thesis, Washington University, 1971), Chapter 2.

[25]Slifman, p. 129.

[26]Lloyd Fisher, "The Harvest Labor Market in California," *Quarterly Journal of Economics*, November 1951, pp. 463-491.

tive of normal working situations, is a curiosity. Most jobs require worker training and cooperative effort and involve the use of expensive equipment. Further, piece-rate systems are not always either feasible or desirable.[27] In their absence, both administrative convenience and the maintenance of worker morale dictate that the wage be more specific to the job than to the individual. Once a wage rate is assigned to a job, the employer naturally seeks to obtain the best possible person for the position.

The employer interest in hiring standards is reinforced by the limited number of ports of entry to the firm. In many industries, it is customary to hire workers only for positions that represent discrete breaks in the skill or responsibility hierarchy. Workers achieve intermediate positions in the hierarchy by promotion from within. Other industries will hire at all levels of the hierarchy. Universities, for instance, appoint academicians at the instructor, assistant, associate, and full professor ranks. Even so, it is customary to reward length of service by giving the current employee an edge over outsiders when desirable openings occur. It is far easier to become a full professor at a leading educational institution—that is, it can be done with less display of merit—if one is already an associate professor at that institution than if one's appointment is elsewhere. Low echelon hiring thus circumscribes the possibilities for filling higher echelon positions. Hiring unskilled workers frequently determines the group from which key semiskilled workers and foremen will eventually be selected. In hiring this year's salesmen, an employer may be selecting a future sales manager. This highly sensible policy of promotion from within means that hiring standards will be pitched higher than are required for the entry job. Quality requirements will reflect the desire for workers capable of ascending the skill and responsibility ladder.

Barring layoffs due to a downturn in business activity, it is not easy to dispose of employees who have accumulated seniority. Most employers are human and have a natural distaste for firing workers. The distaste is reinforced by the negative effect of firings on the morale and loyalty of the remaining workers. It is further reinforced in unionized firms

---

[27]It is not always possible to make employers indifferent to variations in worker performance by variations in worker compensation. If negligence or failure to appear can result in losses that run into multiples of the annual wage, and if employers view some workers as being more likely to err than others, it may not be possible to find a wage sufficiently low to compensate unless losses can be fully bonded.

by collective bargaining clauses that prevent the discharge of employees, who have successfully completed a probationary period, for anything except extreme breaches of efficiency or discipline. The probationary period for manufacturing production workers is quite short, generally varying from 30 to 90 days. In hiring a new employee, the firm is thus making a decision akin to the purchase of a piece of physical capital. It is committing itself to employing the services of a particular individual until his death, retirement, or voluntary resignation, given a sufficiency of demand for labor. This is yet another reason for placing a high premium on the proper selection of workers.

The efficiency and stability of workers can be determined with certainty only after the fact. To improve its prospects for hiring efficient and stable workers, the firm needs cheap and quick techniques that will enable it to preselect the likeliest applicants. It can then subject these applicants to more expensive tests, including the test of the probationary period. Since the firm generally quotes the starting wage, it is not interested in scanning the market widely to find applicants willing to accept lower wages. Rather, it is interested in reducing the number of applicants to manageable proportions, so that it can focus on those who appear sufficiently promising to merit the expense of further investigation.[28] Hence, firms establish hiring standards that are not actual prerequisites for good performance on the job but are proxies for the possession of such desired personal attributes as skill, ambition, self-discipline, ability at social accommodation, and learning capacity. These standards are designed to screen applicants cheaply. At times, educational requirements are authentic prerequisites for satisfactory job performance. Often, though, they are simply low cost screens, either for attributes possessed by those obtaining more education, or for attributes imparted by that education.

Determining an applicant's educational attainment is simple and inexpensive. Everyone is aware that one can be an excellent college undergraduate teacher without having a Ph.D. Some salesmen perform superbly without a college degree. Efficient factory work is performed by persons without high school diplomas. Hiring only workers who have educational credentials is sensible personnel policy, however, if their services can be had at going wage rates, and if they are much more likely than workers without these credentials to perform in the desired fashion, either because of their innate attributes or because of their educational attainment. It is equally sensible to

---

[28]Albert Rees, "Information Networks in Labor Markets," *American Economic Review*, May 1966, p. 561.

relax this screen and to examine less well-educated applicants more closely in a tight labor market, when workers meeting the customary hiring standards can be acquired in the desired period of time only by bidding up wages.

Considerable social concern has been expressed over the maintenance of artificially high hiring standards that prevent workers capable of effective productive performance from finding employment. However, there is little evidence of such non-profit maximizing behavior under high employment circumstances. Hiring standards are relative rather than absolute. One can visualize a hiring queue—the workers regarded as most desirable by employers are ranked at the front, and those regarded as least desirable are ranked at the back. At any given wage, the employer will attempt to hire the most desirable workers—those at the front of the queue. As demand increases, he will raise wages and move farther down the hiring queue. A survey of St. Louis County manufacturers conducted in 1968-69 indicated that the typical manufacturer had three hiring requirements for unskilled and semiskilled workers. Minimum age was by far the most frequently mentioned requirement, reflecting state laws regulating the employment of teenagers in manufacturing. The most important requirement for adult workers was a record of job stability, indicating the desire for an employment relationship sufficiently long to permit the amortization of hiring and training costs. Only a minority of employers had formal educational or police record requirements. Even for these employers, educational requirements were often minimal, and the police record requirement was frequently designed merely to exclude recent felons. The absolute barriers to employment in manufacturing during the highly prosperous 1968-69 period were not very high. As the personnel manager of a large electronics manufacturer expressed it: "We used to insist on high school graduates; now we take eighth grade people. We would like to go back to the high school requirement, but then we wouldn't get anyone."[29] Of course, when labor markets loosened again in 1970-71, employers became more selective.

As we shall see in the next chapter, the level of unemployment is not something immutably determined by natural forces, but to an appreciable extent it is the outcome of conscious or unconscious community choices. Because of an aversion to inflation, our society might well choose in the future as it did in the 1958-64 and 1970-72 periods to live with loose labor markets. Living with loose labor markets means living with high hiring standards. The social cost of high unemployment will then fall disproportionately on those grouped toward the

---

[29]Edward D. Kalachek and John M. Goering, eds., *Transportation and Central City Employment*, p. E-8.

rear of the hiring queue. Since this would involve some inequity, hiring standards could well become a target of social
policy in a high unemployment economy.

CONCLUSIONS

Jobs and workers are highly individualized and evolve over
time as a result of technical change, income growth, the vagaries of public and private taste, and the spread of educational
attainment. The labor market is characterized by continuing
disturbances, pervasive uncertainty over the future, and even
by uncertainty over the contours of the present. In a world of
change, the composition of labor supply can never be ideally
suited to the composition of labor demand. Had the composition
of today's demand for labor been known sufficiently far in advance, a work force could have been generated with a different
set of attributes than that possessed by today's work force.
This hypothetical labor force would have been able to produce
today's output at a lower cost than can the actual labor force.
Since the actual demand and supply for labor are never
well matched, the labor market must reconcile the round hole
with the square peg. A nonstandard worker must be matched with
a nonstandard job. The worker is eligible for a wide range of
jobs, with his potential productivity and earnings varying substantially over this range. The employer will see a large number of job applicants who differ greatly in their potential
productivity and propensity for job stability. Under these
circumstances, unemployment is not necessarily a sign of excess
supply. Vacancies are not necessarily a sign of excess demand.
Rather, both can be investments in search—costs voluntarily
undertaken in the expectation of securing more advantageous employment or employees. At the same time, the unemployment and
vacancy experiences also serve as disciplinary forces. They
alter employer and employee behavior and facilitate the ultimate match between workers and jobs. The workers may find,
given search costs, that the wage or type of work on which he
had set his heart was unrealistic. Accepting a more modest
situation may be the most advantageous option open to him.
Likewise, the persistence of vacancies can force the employer
to compromise between his initial aspirations and reality. The
inability to increase employment to its desired level is a sig-
nal that wages are too low or hiring standards too high.

5

The Theory of Unemployment

The subject of unemployment was introduced in Chapter 4, with emphasis on its role in facilitating the adjustment of labor supply to demand. In this chapter, we explore the theory of unemployment. In the next chapter we shall look at some of the contemporary unemployment problems of the American economy. Our interest in unemployment is not purely intellectual. The individual hardship and the social and economic waste which frequently accompany unemployment are abhorrent. We study unemployment so that we can learn to control it. Unemployment, however, is a complex matter. All unemployment is not socially disruptive or economically wasteful. Some unemployment is a natural concomitant of technical progress and free labor markets, and can be considered socially and economically beneficial. We need a framework for distinguishing the harmful from the beneficial or indifferent instances. Then we can determine the case for remedial social policy and identify an appropriate set of policies.

FULL EMPLOYMENT

A discussion of full employment is the logical starting point for an analysis of unemployment. *Full employment* is a term widely used in popular as well as in technical discussions. The popular or common sense definition of full employment is an employment level sufficiently high that workers can find jobs easily. The essence of this popular definition is captured by the economists' or technical definition. Technically, full employment is a situation in which the demand for labor at going real wages (the money wage divided by the price level) is exactly equal to the supply. There is neither excess demand for labor nor excess supply.

What does a full employment world look like? How do we know full employment when we see it? We will approach this

question by observing the characteristics of full employment
under different hypothetical circumstances. Assume jobs and
workers are homogeneous. Technology, population, the capital
stock, tastes, and money supply are constant. If jobs and
workers are homogeneous, search is highly simplified. Employers are indifferent between homogeneous workers willing to
work at the same wage rates. They are only concerned with
hunting for workers available at lower wages. Locational con-
siderations aside, workers are indifferent between identical
jobs. They search only for higher wage rates. Information
needs are obviously minimal. Necessary information can be
transmitted rapidly and comprehensively. Firms seeking labor
need only advertise their wage rate. Workers seeking jobs
need only check the help wanted ads and select the highest offer. Under such circumstances, competitive pressures would
soon erode wage differentials and the need for protracted
search. Unemployment and vacancies would vanish soon after
arising.

The labor market for this simplified world is adequately
portrayed in Figure 2. Full employment occurs at employment
level OA and real wage rate OB. Everyone willing to work at
that wage rate is employed. All jobs available at that wage
rate are filled. If real wages are higher than OB, labor is
in excess supply. Workers are off their supply schedules since
they cannot sell all the labor they wish at going real wages.
Their frustration results in a downward pressure on wages. Alternatively, a real wage rate less than OB leads to excess demand. Employer bidding for additional workers places an upward
pressure on wages. Full employment is when the labor market
attains equilibrium. Supply and demand are equally balanced
only at full employment. Given our simplified assumptions,

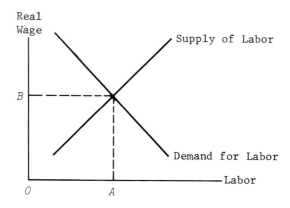

Figure 2. Full Employment with Homogeneous Labor

full employment is easy to identify empirically. Homogeneity
and simple search imply vacancies and unemployment continuously
converging on zero. The constancy of technology, population,
the capital stock, and tastes implies stable real wages. The
constancy of the money supply implies stable money wages. Unemployment converging on zero accompanied by stable money and
real wages would be the hallmark of full employment.

Full employment is not synonymous with maximum employment.
There are people willing to work who do not have jobs. All
persons willing to work but only at a wage rate greater than *OB*
fall into this category. Many a suburban housewife with modest
educational attainments and minimal market skills would be de-
lighted to work if offered a part-time job that was interesting,
highly compensated, nearby, and tension free. Do we wish to
classify such persons as unemployed? They are not doing any
market work, but their joblessness is purely voluntary. Given
current economic inducements, they have opted out of the labor
market. The word *unemployment* seems unfelicitous and should be
avoided here, regardless of whether workers are actively hunting employment or are merely potentially available. The logical alternative would be to consider all jobless persons willing to work under sufficiently favorable circumstances, perhaps
40 to 50 million persons, as unemployed.

Frictional Unemployment

Realism requires us to acknowledge the heterogeneity of
both jobs and workers. If jobs are heterogeneous, workers must
be concerned with net psychic benefits. If workers are heterogeneous, employers must be concerned with labor quality. Information needs become more complex. Wage differentials become
more persistent. Optimum search time becomes lengthier. Full
employment now involves both unemployment and vacancies. The
unemployed are *frictionally* (voluntarily or temporarily) unemployed.

A significant number of persons enter the unemployment
stock each time period. This inflow includes the youth entering the labor market either for the summer or permanently upon
graduation, the housewife seeking work after her children are
grown, and the voluntary quit. It also includes the layoff, an
inevitable casualty of a dynamic economy bombarded by technical
advance, capital-labor ratio changes, and shifts in consumer
tastes. This inflow, together with positive search time, results in frictional unemployment. The distinguishing characteristic of frictionality is not the channel of entry into the unemployment stock but rather the voluntariness of the stay.

The voluntary aspect of frictional unemployment is seen
clearly from the perspective of the neoclassical theory of job

search. The frictionally unemployed worker, aware of the probability distribution of job offers to which he will be exposed,
selects the combination of acceptance wage and expected duration of unemployment that maximizes the discounted value of his
expected net future stream of income and psychic benefits.
This worker could always have reduced the duration of unemployment to zero by selecting a sufficiently low acceptance wage,
though such behavior would be rather foolish.

The concept of voluntariness becomes a bit muddied, though
still remaining valid, once we account for the realities of the
job hunt. Frictional unemployment should not require omniscience or well-organized and nonneurotic decision making. Workers who lack a priori knowledge of their market prospects and
use search to define the range of options are frictionally unemployed; so are workers whose behavior can be explained by the
aspiration-level hypothesis. At any moment, some workers will
be seeking jobs in specific occupations, areas, or at wage
rates that are unrealistic, but as the labor market is more
fully explored, these demands will be scaled down. A worker is
frictionally unemployed if he arrives at an acceptance wage
that results in a substantially positive probability of reemployment per unit of time, even though he began with unrealistic aspirations.

Unemployment is frictional if it results from the effort
to hunt the most preferable of attainable options. This option
will not necessarily be the highest possible wage or the same
as the last wage. Sometimes it will be higher and sometimes
lower. It doesn't matter whether the decision that a lower
wage is income maximizing is made at the beginning of the
search or after the search has progressed for some time. It
doesn't matter whether the job hunt is prolonged by ineptitude
or neurosis, nor whether the hunt is comfortable or psychologically and financially onerous. Unemployment is voluntary and
frictional if the following conditions are met: (1) It results
from the hunt for a preferable option; (2) It could always be
terminated by accepting a less preferable option; (3) The worker eventually arrives at an acceptance wage that results in a
positive probability of employment per unit of time; (4) Securing work does not lead to the layoff of an employed worker. No
change in the parameters of the economy are required to termi-
nate a spell of frictional unemployment. If the continuing
life cycle changes, and personal vagaries and disturbances that
lead to frictional unemployment were all suspended by the wave
of a magic wand, the frictionally unemployed would complete
their job hunt and find employment, and frictional unemployment
would disappear. Even when the stock of frictional unemployment is constant, its composition is everchanging.

The concept of frictional unemployment is illustrated in
Figure 3; the labor supply schedule is decomposed into two com-

ponents. During any time period, some persons will be offering
work time. Others will be in or entering the unemployment
stock. Their stay there will depend on the conditions set for
reemployment. The S_L schedule represents the supply of work
time. The S_{L+U} schedule represents the supply of both work
time and search effort. The distance between the two schedules
represents worker search effort. Employers confront an analogous situation. Each time period, new vacancies arise. It is
more profitable at times to engage in search rather than to
raise wages or lower hiring standards immediately. Consequently, the demand for labor can be decomposed into two components.
The D_L schedule represents the number of jobs employers are
willing to fill. The D_{L+V} schedule represents the number of
jobs and of vacancies that employers will offer. The distance
between the two schedules represents employer search effort.
All demand and supply schedules are functions of the real wage
rate.

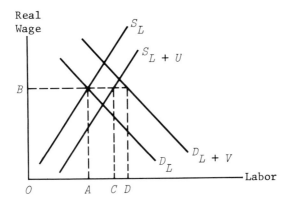

Figure 3. Frictional Unemployment

In Figure 3, full employment occurs at employment level
OA and real wage rate OB. However, this is only part of the
story. Given inflows to unemployment and the average duration
of search, workers must offer to fill OC jobs in any period to
obtain OA jobs. The difference, AC, is frictional unemployment. Given the inflow of vacancies and the average duration
of search, employers must offer OD jobs to fill OA jobs. The
difference, AD, is job vacancies. The literature generally assumes that vacancies and unemployment are equal at full employment. This assumption is incorrect. Full employment requires
only a clearing of the labor market. There should be no pressure on wages due to excess demand or excess supply. This con-
dition is satisfied when vacancies and unemployment are both

desired. At full employment, workers and employers prefer to
engage in hunts of AC and AD rather than to lower their aspirations.[1]

We have purchased insight by ruthlessly abstracting from
the complexities of the real world. In truth, there is no
single wage rate that clears the market. There is no single
labor market. There are many different interrelated submarkets
that clear at different wage rates. Electricians, carpenters,
dishwashers, maids, economists, and engineers all earn different wage rates. The labor markets in which they compete may be
national, regional, or local. Within a market, wage rates may
vary depending on the quality of the worker. National problems
can be analyzed effectively only at the aggregative level. To
proceed, we must suppress the great diversity that characterizes reality and speak of the labor market and the wage rate.
Figure 3 is a valuable fiction engaged in for pedagogical convenience.

Measuring Full Employment

At any moment, the economy will have a full employment position, sometimes referred to as the *natural rate of unemployment*. In Figure 3, it is graphically portrayed by AC, frictional unemployment, divided by OC, the full employment labor
force. The natural rate is an appealing target, even though
its attainment will not solve all social problems. All those
willing to work at the going real wage surely should be en-
titled to jobs. But what is the natural rate? Is it three,
four, or six percent unemployment? Given static assumptions,
full employment is easy to identify. It is the unemployment
rate at which money and real wages are stable. This easy iden-
tifiability disappears in a real world of economic growth,
varying monetary policies, and market imperfections. Neutral
technical advance and increases in the capital stock raise real
wages. Population growth lowers them. The equilibrium value
of the money wage depends on monetary policy. Through time,
wages change continuously, whether or not the economy is at
full employment. In addition, the wages of over 18 million
workers are determined at least nominally through collective
bargaining. We must conclude that real or money wage changes
are not an unequivocal guide to the supply-demand balance in
the labor market. Stable money wages are not proof of full employment. Money wage increases do not demonstrate an excess
demand for labor.

---

[1]See Melvin W. Reder, "The Theory of Frictional Unemployment,"
Economica, February 1969, pp. 1-28.

Full employment is characterized by positive unemployment and an indeterminate rate of change in the money and real wage. How can it be identified? Some economists have attempted to estimate frictionality directly. For instance, Simler equates frictional unemployment with durations of 14 weeks or less, and emerges with a two percent estimate.[2] Most spells of frictional unemployment should be short. Most workers are located in major metropolitan areas containing a large number of job opportunities. For those who own automobiles, and most workers do, intercity transportation is quick and inexpensive. It should be possible to canvass an immense number of jobs in several months. Nonetheless, short duration and frictional unemployment are not synonymous. Some workers may find a very long search a profitable investment. Others may be stranded in a geographically isolated area by a plant closedown or find their skills obsolete as a result of technical change. They must make the agonizing decision to relocate or to accept wages considerably lower than those to which they have become accustomed. Some people make difficult decisions rapidly; others only after they have been chastened by time. A Bureau of Labor Statistics study indicated that labor force entry and reentry, job quitting, and seasonal fluctuations resulted during the prosperity years of 1955-57 in an unemployment rate of two percent. This is, however, a lower bound estimate, since it fails to account for the normal amount of layoffs during a prosperity year.[3]

Other economists have used a historical comparison-relative price stability gauge. President Kennedy's Council of Economic Advisers formally articulated four percent as full employment (taking account of both frictional and structural unemployment) and as the goal of national economic policy.[4] In embracing four percent, the Council was guided by historical experience and value judgment. In the preceding dozen years, the economy had twice attained four percent with inflationary pressures which were considered either tolerable or due to special circumstances. Four percent had proved attainable and probably was noninflationary. Hence, it was full employment.

---

[2]Norman J. Simler, "Long Term Unemployment, The Structural Hypothesis and Public Policy," *American Economic Review*, December 1964, pp. 985-1001.

[3]U.S. Department of Labor, Bureau of Labor Statistics, "The Extent and Nature of Frictional Unemployment," Study Paper No. 6, Materials Prepared for the Joint Economic Committee, 86th Congress, 1st Session, November 19, 1959.

[4]*Economic Report of the President Together with The Annual Report of the Council of Economic Advisers* (Washington: U.S. Government Printing Office, 1962), pp. 46-47.

Likewise, in arguing during 1971 for a higher target, Secretary of the Treasury Connally noted that four percent had never been achieved in peacetime without inflation. This price stability gauge may be politically palatable. However, it has little to do with the availability of job opportunities, and hence is technically inappropriate. The problem is that we can discuss full employment but we do not know how to measure it. In Chapter 6, we shall see how this lack of operational knowledge beclouds the formulation of public policy.

To complicate matters further, the natural rate will not be historically constant. Frictional unemployment is the product of full employment values of the inflows to unemployment (from layoffs, quits, discharges, and labor force entrances) and the average job hunting interval. These factors are all susceptible to secular and irregular changes. The quit rate and population growth in the labor market entry age groups both vary considerably over time. There will be more frictional unemployment in a year when two million boys reach their eighteenth birthdays than in a year when this group is smaller. Productivity gains also show considerable year to year variation. Productivity advance results in the creation of jobs in some industries and the destruction of jobs in others. Since rapid productivity change generates both new job vacancies and new layoffs, it will generally lead to high frictional unemployment.

Job hunting time must also be altered by improvements in the speed, reach, and availability of transportation and communications networks. These improvements have led to an ability to scan the market more rapidly and hence to shorter spells of frictional unemployment. As we have seen, more liberal welfare and unemployment compensation benefits should have the opposite effect. The length of the job hunt is also affected by the factor bias of technical change. If newly created jobs closely approximate the qualifications and interests of job hunters, matching can proceed expeditiously. On the other hand, if vacancies call for highly trained white collar workers and the unemployed are low skilled blue collar workers, the job hunt will be more protracted, since matching may require changes in relative wages, job redesign, skill level dilution, and career redirection.

Frictional unemployment will not remain stable, given this great variability in its determinants. A fluctuating level of frictional unemployment can lead the monetary and fiscal authorities into serious error. If they are attempting to maintain full employment, an undetected rise in frictional unemployment will result in inflation. An undetected decline will result in an underambitious use of monetary-fiscal policy and in the toleration of more unemployment than is socially necessary.

Frictional Unemployment and Public Policy

Monetary and fiscal policies are appropriate techniques for driving unemployment to the frictional level, but not for coping with frictional unemployment. Overly high frictional unemployment calls for labor market programs to improve the match between jobs and workers, to speed the flow of information, and to facilitate mobility. If some of the frictionally unemployed—for example, the technically obsolete—are bearing an inequitable burden, the solution is to create programs for retraining and upgrading skills. Such programs represent public investment in human capital. They should be instituted or expanded (since we already have a handsome array of such programs) if they satisfy the benefit-cost criteria applicable to government investment programs. First, the net reduction in frictional unemployment resulting from various amounts and types of labor market expenditure should be determined. Second, the social value of these reductions should be estimated. (The social value would be the sum of the additional streams of output resulting from lower unemployment and of the social premiums attached to reducing unemployment because it is bad in itself or has adverse social consequences.) Third, the highest discount rate, which equates these future streams of real and imputed returns to the cost of labor market policy, should be discovered. This will be the rate of return on labor market policy as a function of expenditure for this purpose. Labor market policy is pursued until this rate of return is brought into equality with the rate of return on other investments.

DEMAND DEFICIENCY UNEMPLOYMENT

Frictional unemployment is consistent with full employment and is voluntary. Involuntary unemployment occurs when the economy falls short of full employment. Such unemployment is called *demand deficiency unemployment*, since it is due to a deficiency of aggregate demand. Workers are unemployed because there are not enough jobs to go around. Insufficient jobs are a macroeconomic disorder that can be explained only by a macroeconomic model. We will construct a highly simplified version of such a model for the labor and commodity markets. (This model will further elucidate the labor demand schedules shown in Figures 2 and 3.) It will focus on the short run by assuming a constant level of technology and a capital stock of fixed size. Capital and homogeneous labor will be the only inputs to the production process. Although the amount of capital is fixed, its embodiment is flexible. Capital can be congealed at will into different types and sizes of machinery.

With the capital stock fixed and labor input variable, the law of diminishing returns is applicable. As additional increments of labor are employed, output increases, first perhaps at a steadily growing rate, but then at a steadily diminishing rate.[5] This variation of output or total physical product (*TPP*) with labor input is shown in the top part of Figure 4. Earth excavation provides an excellent illustration of the law of diminishing returns. The limited capital available might be fashioned into a large shovel. With such a shovel, one worker might dig perhaps ten cubic feet of earth per period. Alternatively, if two shovels were constructed, each would necessarily be smaller. Consequently, adding a second worker to the project would not double the amount of earth excavated. Each worker would produce less per hour than would a single worker with a larger shovel. After all, each worker has less capital to assist him. Two workers using smaller shovels could perhaps dig 18 cubic feet. The marginal physical product (*MPP_L*) of the second worker, the addition to total output resulting from his employment, will then be eight cubic feet. The equivalent of eight cubic feet is all that an employer would pay this worker, or the first worker, with whom he is perfectly interchangeable. Stated otherwise, if the wage rate is eight cubic feet per period, the firm will congeal its capital into two shovels and hire two workers. If the wage rate is between eight and ten cubic feet, the firm will congeal its capital into one shovel only and hire one worker. Since we live in a monetary economy, we will seek the monetary analogue of this barter relationship.

In a monetary economy, profit maximizing employers are interested in a worker's contribution to revenue rather than to production. They will carry output to the point at which rising marginal costs (*MC*) are equal to marginal revenue. Assuming perfect competition prevails, marginal revenue will equal price (*P*). Employers will then produce at the point where $P = MC$. Labor being the only variable input, marginal cost is obtained by dividing the wage rate (*W*) by the *MPP_L*. If W is $10 and the marginal worker adds 5 units to total output, $MC = \$2$. If $P = MC$ and $MC = W/MPP$ then $W = P \cdot MPP_L$. The statement that profit maximizing employers produce where $P = MC$ is

---

[5]This assumption is traditional and convenient but not necessary. The alternative short run assumption would be a capital stock fixed in size and composition. If the capital stock is already congealed into machinery, production coefficients may be quite rigid. The short run demand schedule for labor could be perfectly horizontal over the relevant range. As the reader proceeds, he may note that this change in assumption would not materially affect the outcome of the analysis.

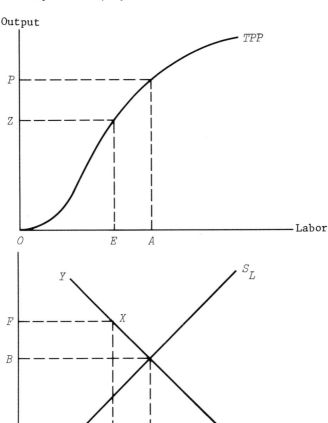

Figure 4.   Demand Deficiency Unemployment

equivalent to the statement that they hire labor up to the
point at which the wage equals the value of the marginal product. A further rearrangement of terms yields $W/P = MPP_L$. Employers hire workers up to the point at which the marginal
physical product equals the real wage. The MPP_L schedule is
then the demand schedule for labor. It is shown in the bottom
half of Figure 4.[6] This schedule describes the amount of employment firms will offer at any real wage rate. It is drawn

---

[6]More precisely, the downward sloping segment of the MPP_L
schedule, which lies below the average physical product of
labor, is shown and is the demand schedule for labor. An

on the assumption, normally valid for perfectly competitive markets, that entrepreneurs can sell all they can produce at going prices.

The demand schedule summarizes desired behavior on one side of the market. The other side is described in Figure 4 by a positively sloped supply schedule of labor. This schedule indicates the amount of labor workers will provide at various real wage rates. As we have seen, these two schedules determine the real wage rate (*OB*) and employment level (*OA*) consistent with full employment. However, full employment is not inevitable. Employment is subject to more than labor market influences. The labor market is not a law unto itself; it is just one of the economy's key markets. Full employment requires a real wage of *OB*, but this real wage is not sufficient to guarantee full employment. The labor market will not clear unless the commodity and financial markets are also in equilibrium.

So long as technology is constant and the capital stock fixed, output and employment are uniquely related. As illustrated in Figure 4, the production of any specified output requires a particular level of employment. Likewise, the determination of employment in the bottom half of Figure 4 fixes the output level in the top half of the figure. At full employment, *OA* workers will be employed and will produce an output of *OP*. We will refer to this crucial level of activity, the normal outer boundary of a society's production possibilities, as *potential output*. At any moment of time, potential output is a constant, determined by technology, the size of the capital stock, and the labor supply function.

Full employment, once achieved, will persist only if firms can sell potential output period after period, engaging in neither unwanted accumulation nor depletion of inventories. The expectations underlying full employment production will be satisfied only if aggregate demand for goods and services is equal to potential output. Aggregate demand is the sum of government expenditures, personal consumption expenditures, gross private domestic investment, and net exports. Ignoring net exports for convenience, aggregate demand will be treated as a function of real income, the interest rate, real wealth, and exogenously determined government expenditure and tax decisions.

The commodity market is depicted in Figure 5. Output and income are measured on the horizontal axis; aggregate demand is

---

[6]cont.   employer would never operate to the left of this point since he would be paying workers more than their average product and would be incurring losses that could be averted by closing down. The MPP_L schedule is, of course, the first derivative of the TPP_L schedule.

measured on the vertical axis. The aggregate demand schedules
are drawn on the assumption of constancy in real wealth, interest rate, and government expenditures. They show how demand
varies with the level of real income. They are positively
sloped since higher real income leads to higher personal consumption expenditures. The 45-degree line is the locus of
points at which aggregate demand and output are equal. Potential output is depicted by a straight line perpendicular to the
output axis at OP.

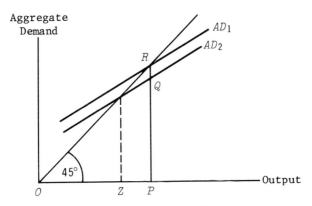

Figure 5.   The Commodity Market

Suppose the aggregate demand curve, AD_1, intersects potential output at point R on the 45-degree line. This intersec-
tion indicates that expenditure units (consumers, business, and
government) are willing to spend 100 cents of every dollar of
income generated at full employment. Ex ante investment plus
government expenditures exactly equal ex ante savings plus
taxes at full employment. Businessmen will sell precisely what
they have produced. In a static world, they would have no inducement either to expand or to contract production. Full employment would be consistent with commodity market equilibrium
and so would persist unless the system were given some external
shock (so long as financial markets, whose portrayal we abstract from here for the sake of simplicity, are also in equilibrium). On the other hand, it is quite possible that aggregate demand will equal output only at some production level
less than OP. This is illustrated by AD_2, which intersects the
45-degree line at an output of OZ. If businessmen were now to
produce OP, aggregate demand would be only PQ. A deflationary
gap of QR would emerge. Inventories would accumulate and output would be reduced. Demand is only sufficient to justify an
output level of OZ. At this output level, there will be demand
deficiency unemployment.

The labor demand schedule in Figure 4 was constructed on
the assumption that firms could sell all that they could produce at going prices. This assumption has been invalidated.
Consequently, the demand schedule is no longer fully operative.[7] Disequilibrium in the commodity market has fed back
into disequilibrium in the labor market. Firms hire only the
amount of labor needed to produce OZ. The result is an income
constrained demand schedule such as YXE. Demand deficiency unemployment has arisen even though the real wage is at its equilibrium value. Commodity rather than labor market imbalances
are to blame. It is helpful to think of a short run chain of
causation going from aggregate demand to actual output to employment. At a real wage rate of OB, indeed at any real wage
rate between zero and OF, firms will provide employment of
only OE. Commodity and labor market relationships will admittedly be unstable. Given any real wage below OF, businessmen
will continuously be tempted to increase output. However,
given aggregate demand, expansion will result in inventories
piling up and in subsequent retrenchment.

Equilibrating Mechanisms

If demand is income constrained, workers will be forced
off their supply schedule. They will be attempting to supply
more labor at the going real wage than employers are willing
to purchase. Downward flexibility in money wages can be expected. Assume that wages fall without limit in the presence
of excess supply. Will the underutilization of labor and other
productive capacity be a highly transitory and self-correcting
event? Will the system hunt and find full employment? Can involuntary unemployment be a serious problem in a world of flexible wages? To answer these questions, we have the benefit of
the classical-Keynesian exchange over the equilibrating role of
wage flexibility. The classical position that equilibrium occurs only at full employment given wage flexibility emerged
victorious from this debate. The victory, however, was a
Pyrrhic one, since the requirements for wage flexibility are so
onerous that they exceed realistic expectation. Demand deficiency unemployment is a disequilibrium occurrence, but the
disequilibrium can persist through time.
    Extreme wage flexibility is required because lower wages
lead to full employment through financial and product consequences rather than through labor market consequences. A

---

[7]See the incisive analysis in Chapter XIII of Don Patinkin,
Money, Interest and Prices, second edition (New York: Harper
and Row, Publishers, 1965).

simple logical exercise will demonstrate this point. Assume
the aggregate demand schedule AD_2 and the output level OZ.
Involuntary unemployment exists and leads to wage reductions.
Assume that these wage reductions do not shift the aggregate
demand schedule. Lower money wages mean lower marginal costs.
Profit maximizing firms are spurred to price reductions and to
output and employment increases. However, with the aggregate
demand function constant, output increases lead to undesired
inventory accumulation. These increases will then be transitory. Prior to the wage reduction, output levels greater than
OZ were not tenable since demand was not adequate to clear the
market of the goods and services produced. The consumption
expenditures of the workers hired to produce output beyond OZ
were not adequate to justify their employment since the marginal propensity to consume is less than one. Wage reduction and
the resulting temporary flurry of employment increases do not
change this fact. Aggregate demand is still deficient at any
output level in excess of OZ. Output increases beyond OZ can
be sustained only if the aggregate demand schedule is shifted
upward.

The financial and product market repercussions of aggregate wage declines do lead to such a shift. Wage declines result in price declines. They, in turn, reduce the nominal
money balances needed for transaction purposes. The liberated
money balances flow into the bond market, raising bond prices
and lowering interest rates. Investment, an important component of aggregate demand, is affected by interest rates. Lower
interest rates increase investment outlays and thus raise the
aggregate demand function. If the interest elasticity of demand for money balance is low and the interest elasticity of
the investment function is high, this may be sufficient to restore full employment. The aggregate demand schedule may be
shifted upward to intersect point R. However, this is not an
inevitable outcome. The increase in investment will be stymied
if the economy encounters a liquidity trap or a perfectly interest inelastic segment of the investment function.

Wage and price reductions also shift the aggregate demand
schedule upward by increasing private sector real wealth. To
see why, we must examine the relationship between wealth and
consumption. Individuals can be assumed to have a desired
level of real nonhuman wealth. This target level of wealth is
dependent on tastes, age, the interest rate, and income. Saving out of current income is a response to a discrepancy between the actual and desired level of wealth. People save to
bring their actual wealth position in line with their desired
position. The saver foregoes the utility that could be obtained from current consumption. In return, he receives utility from the prospect of assured future consumption and from
the various other options opened by a wealth position. The

individual selects a savings rate at which the marginal utility
derived from current consumption is equal to the marginal utility derived from wealth increments. Suppose that an individual's wealth were appreciably increased, his income being unaffected. The marginal utility of wealth would decline; the
marginal utility of current consumption would be unchanged. A
utility maximizing household would respond by increasing current consumption. Wealth increases thus shift the consumption
function upward. There should exist an addition to personal
wealth sufficiently large that it deters any saving out of current income. There should exist an even larger wealth increment that would encourage a consumption level in excess of
current income.

Price declines increase the real value of wealth denominated in fixed sums. As prices fall, the real value of mort-
gages, fiat money, bonds, and other loan instruments increases.
The discrepancy between actual and desired wealth is reduced.
Consumption and aggregate demand rise at every level of income.
Of course, most wealth instruments denominated in fixed sums
are also debt instruments. Debtors become poorer at the same
rate that creditors become wealthier. For private instruments,
the favorable consumption effect of the wealth increases of
debt holders is offset by the unfavorable consumption effect of
wealth decreases on debt emitters. Government bonds and money
are a different matter. Declines in the general price level
increase the real wealth of private holders of these liabili-
ties while worsening the government's wealth position. Since
it is normally assumed that government expenditures are unaffected by the government's real wealth position, the net impact
of price declines is an expansion of aggregate demand.[8] At
some critical level of private real wealth, consumption will be
sufficiently great to ensure that aggregate demand equals full
employment income. If wages and prices are flexible downward
in the face of excess supply, and capable of falling without
limit, this critical level of private wealth will ultimately be
attained. This happy outcome is certain unless deflation results in a wave of bankruptcies which demoralize private wealth
holders, or unless consumers perpetually postpone expenditures
in anticipation of still lower prices.

---

[8]Taxpayers may perceive that the higher real value of government bonds entails higher real interest rates and hence higher
real taxes over time. There will be no real wealth effect if
the change in tax obligations is fully discounted. On the
other hand, money is not a true debt of the government. An increase in the real value of the privately held money stock represents an unequivocal increase in private real wealth.

Unfortunately, the wage and price declines necessary to restore the system to full employment may be extremely large. It might be necessary to double or triple real wealth to achieve the desired consumption response, and government bonds and fiat money represent only a modest fraction of real wealth. A considerable number of economists believe that aggregate wages are flexible downward. No one believes, nor is there reason to believe, that they will fall rapidly or to very low levels. During the decade of the Great Depression, the unemployment rate averaged 18 percent. Manufacturing wages fell 20 percent between 1929 and 1933, but then rose steeply. In 1939, they were actually 12 percent higher than in 1929. Money wages continued to rise during each of the five post World War II recessions. We conclude without serious hesitation that money wages are not sufficiently flexible to prevent the occurrence and protracted persistence of demand deficiency unemployment.

It should now be clear why frictional unemployment is regarded as voluntary and demand deficiency unemployment as involuntary. The frictionally unemployed worker can always obtain a job promptly and without ousting an incumbent by the simple expedient of lowering his acceptance wage. A worker unemployed because of demand deficiency can secure employment by offering to work for less, but he will be depriving a competitor of a job. In the event of demand deficiency, across the board rather than individual wage declines are required to increase total employment. These general wage declines may have to be astronomically large since their effectiveness depends on circuitous and uncertain macroeconomic processes.

A Dynamic Perspective

The analysis so far has been static. However, demand deficiency unemployment is essentially a dynamic problem best viewed from a dynamic perspective. Potential output continuously increases in response to rightward shifts in the demand and supply schedules of labor. Augmented investment in human beings, a larger stock of physical capital, or neutral advances in technology all shift the demand curve to the right. Rates of return on investment in human and nonhuman capital are reasonably high, and historically unprecedented sums are being devoted to research and development. Consequently, each year sees new advances in educational attainment, in the capital stock, and in technology. Growth in the working age population currently proceeding at better than two percent annually shifts the supply curve to the right. The result is growth in potential output at an annual rate somewhat higher than four percent.

An economy at full employment will stay there only if aggregate demand grows as rapidly as potential output. Aggregate

demand is forced to run on a fast track. The investment expenditures that increase potential output also have a favorable effect on aggregate demand. Still, any net investment increases
potential output. Only an increase in net investment expands
aggregate demand. There is no automatic self-equilibrating
mechanism that guarantees that aggregate demand and potential
output always grow at the same rate. The economy is continuously vulnerable to demand deficiency unemployment.

The most obvious instances occur during recessions, when
sales and output decline and remain below earlier peaks. Then,
the inadequacy of job opportunities is obvious. Job deficiency,
however, is not restricted to recessions. It occurs whenever
aggregate demand falls short of potential output. In the early
1960s, the gross national product, industrial production, retail sales, corporate profits, and employment rose continuously
to record levels. Unemployment remained at what was regarded
as an unsatisfactory 5.5 percent rate. Editorial writers found
a serious paradox in this combination of record level economic
activity and high unemployment. Now we know better. Record
levels of output and employment are consistent with high unemployment. During the early 1960s, aggregate demand was growing
as rapidly as potential output. The equivalence of these two
growth rates was sufficient to keep the unemployment rate constant. An economy at a four percent unemployment rate would
have remained there. Instead, the American economy started the
early 1960s at a 5.5 percent unemployment rate and its growth
performance kept it there. To approach four percent, aggregate
demand would have had to grow substantially more rapidly than
potential output.[9]

---

[9]Note that a 1.5 percent increase in output attained instantaneously is not sufficient to reduce unemployment by 1.5 percentage points. Output increases are not translated into commensurate unemployment reductions due to the inverse correlation
between the unemployment rate and the size of the labor force,
the length of the work week, and the effective utilization of
worker skills. Arthur M. Okun, former Chairman of the President's Council of Economic Advisers, estimates that a 3.2 percent rise in output is necessary to reduce the unemployment
rate by one percentage point. See "Potential GNP: Its Measurement and Significance," *1962 Proceedings of the Business and
Economic Statistics Section of the American Statistical Association.*

Monetary and Fiscal Policy

Demand deficiency unemployment was a critical and seemingly unsolvable problem during the 1930s. Since then, we have
developed an arsenal of monetary and fiscal tools for coping
with it. Monetary policy, by increasing the availability of
credit and lowering interest rates, stimulates investment in
plant and equipment, in new housing, and in consumer durables.
Government expenditures on goods and services directly raise
aggregate demand, unless they discourage an equivalent amount
of private expenditures. Like any other stimulus, government
expenditures have multiplier-accelerator effects. Tax reductions, depending on their incidence, raise disposable income
and consumption, or else directly spur investment by increasing
its profitability. There always exists some combination of
money supply growth, government expenditures, and tax rates
capable of driving the system to full employment. It is technically feasible to prevent protracted periods of high demand
deficiency unemployment.
    Given the vicissitudes we have experienced in the past,
this capability is no small achievement. Still, containment
and elimination are different matters. Although we can contain
demand deficiency unemployment, we cannot realistically expect
to eliminate it. The mediocrity of our predictive models, the
lethargies of the legislative process, an aversion to inflation,
and response lags prevent monetary and fiscal tools from being
used as fine tuning instruments. They can be deployed effectively against only gross problems. Demand deficiency unemployment could be prevented only if we were able to predict the
future accurately. We would have to predict the moment when
potential output would begin to outpace aggregate demand and
then base preventive policy on this prediction. Short run
econometric forecasting models provide indispensable guidance
to economic planners. Nonetheless, their ability to predict
the future is less than awesome. If we respond to every prediction of demand deficiency, we will respond to some incorrect
predictions. The resulting unnecessary monetary and fiscal
stimulation will lead to excess demand for labor and to wage
and price increases. All demand deficiency unemployment can be
avoided only if we accept some inflation, and inflation is politically unpopular. Congress will not respond to predictions.
It will act only when prodded by the presence of demand deficiency unemployment. Hence, some demand deficiency unemployment must be endured.
    Even recognizing demand deficiency will not set policy in-
to motion immediately. It takes time to frame, debate, and
pass appropriate legislation. Fiscal policy affects the distribution of income and the allocation of resources between
private and social purposes. It is inevitably controversial.

Liberals seek to use fiscal policy to increase government expenditures, inaugurate new social programs, and enlarge the
public sector. Conservatives see the need to stimulate demand
as an opportunity for reducing taxes. Since these matters must
be thrashed out, there is a substantial lag between the perception of demand deficiency and changes in fiscal policy. Monetary policy is determined by the Federal Reserve System and can
be altered more easily. The Federal Reserve can change policy
at will and rapidly implement its decisions. However, there
are further, lengthy lags between the institution of monetary
or fiscal policy and its effect on the level of economic activity. Time is required before improved credit conditions lead
to more borrowing, and before more borrowing leads to more output and employment. Likewise, federal monies for the construction of highways, hospitals, or sewage plants are not spent in
the month of their authorization, but over a period of years,
as plans are made, land purchased, contracts let, and construction initiated. Although tax reductions can be implemented
rapidly, consumer response is often delayed.

Eliminating demand deficiency unemployment is thus infea-
sible. The best we can expect is that judicious recourse to
monetary and fiscal policy will keep bouts of demand deficiency unemployment infrequent, of relatively brief duration,
and of modest magnitude.

STRUCTURAL UNEMPLOYMENT

So far, the analytic framework has been tidy. However,
our only knowledge of real world unemployment comes from official statistics. The analytic framework must help explain the
unemployment these statistics record. This requires the development of another and rather imprecise concept. As discussed
in Chapter 2, a worker is classified as unemployed by the federal government if he did not work during the survey week, made
specific efforts to find a job within the preceding four weeks,
and was available for work during the survey week. The CPS
(Current Population Survey) does not collect information from
respondents on reservation wages or market productivity. A job
hunter will be classified as unemployed even if his reservation wage is so unrealistic that it reduces his probability
of finding work to zero. The official statistics should not
be criticized for these omissions. It is unlikely that useful
information could be collected on reservation wages or market
productivity.

Still, the official definition of unemployment is quite
different from the definitions utilized in economic models.
Economists classify as unemployed only those job hunters who
are willing, immediately or after some search, to work at the

going real wage for their skills. A bridge is needed between the economic and the official definitions of unemployment. The concept of *structural unemployment* provides the bridge. A worker who is persistently unwilling or unable to work at the going wage but who nonetheless appears in the official statistics is structurally unemployed. The structurally unemployed are a small component of a group we earlier chose to classify as being realistically out of the labor market. Graphically, anyone to the right of the OC on the S_{L+U} schedule in Figure 3, who is classified as unemployed in the official definition, is structurally unemployed.

Structural unemployment can result from unrealistic job aspirations. A worker's reservation wage may be higher than his marginal product. Occupational or geographic reservations can also be unrealistic. A worker may insist on a mining job in his home town even after the ore deposits there have become uneconomic to mine. In these instances, structural unemployment is voluntary. It is the limiting case of frictional unemployment. A frictionally unemployed worker makes the adjustments that result in a positive probability per unit of time of reemployment; a structurally unemployed worker does not. Other troublesome but unlikely situations will also be classified as structural unemployment. The statutory minimum wage or a union negotiated wage may exceed the marginal product of some workers, thus leading to unemployment. Fixed production coefficients and factor shortages may result in some workers having zero marginal products. Given nonwage costs of employment, these workers will be hired only if willing to work at negative wages. If capital-labor coefficients are fixed, full employment of the capital stock may be reached while labor is still in excess supply. Suppose that production always required one worker and one machine. The machine could not be operated with less than one worker, whereas more than one made no contribution whatsoever to output. Let there be 60 machines and 80 workers. Twenty workers are then completely redundant.

Fixed skill coefficients represent another possible source of mischief. Full employment of the skilled labor force may be reached while there are still excess supplies of unskilled labor. Suppose the typical production process required precisely two skilled and one unskilled workers. There is no need for more than one unskilled worker and no possibility of operating with less than two skilled workers. Let the labor force consist of 40 skilled and 40 unskilled workers. In this example, 20 unskilled workers are completely redundant. They cannot find employment at any positive wage.

In all these theoretically possible situations, structural unemployment is involuntary. However, such situations hardly seem applicable to the American economy. Only one-fourth of the labor force is unionized and the minimum wage laws are not applicable to the entire work force, although their coverage is steadily growing. Workers excluded from some sectors by high union or minimum wages can find employment elsewhere. Union negotiated wages and minimum wage laws may aggravate spells of frictional unemployment but they are unlikely to result in unemployability. Capital shortage may exist in many areas of the world, but certainly not in the United States. Skill coefficients are undoubtedly fixed at any moment. Still, there is impressive evidence of employers' ability to upgrade workers and to redesign and dilute job content, given any time in which to adjust to factor shortages or changes in relative factor prices. For all practical purposes, whatever structural unemployments exist must be traceable to persistently unrealistic worker aspirations.

Structural unemployment is bottleneck unemployment. It is a hard core phenomenon, normally not susceptible to the passage of time or to the expansion of aggregate demand. Aggregate demand increases will not reduce structural unemployment, but will be completely dissipated in higher levels of money wages and prices. Permanent employment can be found for the structurally unemployed only if there is a removal of barriers or an increase or transformation of the appropriate inputs. If the minimum or reservation wage exceeds marginal productivity, the minimum wage can be rescinded, or workers can be counselled to more realistic aspirations. Otherwise, investments in training, health, or in psychological counselling will be required to raise productivity. If there is a shortage of skilled workers, additional ones must be trained. If workers are immobile, they must be bribed to mobility or else activities must be located near them. The augmentation of human capital will normally be the appropriate policy response to structural unemployment.

Measuring Structural Unemployment

How much structural unemployment do we experience? Statistics on the duration of unemployment should provide some clues. A structurally unemployed worker seems destined to endure a lifetime spell of unemployment if the conditions that led to his problem persist. However, these conditions may alter due to changes in demand and technology, investments in human and physical capital, and the retirement or mobility of labor force members holding down jobs that the structurally unemployed are qualified to fill. Consequently, structural unemployment spells should be long but not necessarily synonymous with lifetime unemployment. The interpretation of unemployment spells is complex since they may be quite protracted, even in the absence of structural problems. Spells of three to six months or even longer may simply reflect poor search tactics or

the slow adaptation of reservation wages to market realities.
Periods of economic slack result in lengthier unemployment
spells for all job hunters. If workers were homogeneous, all
the unemployed would have the same probability per unit of time
of securing employment. This probability would be the hiring
rate divided by the unemployment stock. It would be low if
the hiring rate were low or the unemployment stock large.
Chance would then result in some workers receiving jobs immediately while others suffered onerously long waits.[10] An appro-
priately long cutoff duration will avoid mistakenly classifying
too many workers as structurally unemployed simply because
their joblessness occurred simultaneously with a period of economic slack. Such an unemployment duration can only be roughly
identified as longer than six months but shorter than a lifetime.

The Department of Labor publishes data on the number of
persons experiencing six months or more of consecutive unemployment. These long duration unemployed have accounted for between 0.1 percent of the labor force in 1951-53 and 1.1 percent
in 1961. During the past quarter of a century, they have accounted for 0.5 percent of the civilian labor force. Some of
these workers were structurally unemployed. On the other hand,
the peaking of long duration unemployment during such a recession year as 1961 indicates that many unemployed were the vic-
tims of demand deficiency.

Norman J. Simler has developed a convincing econometric
model for explaining long durations of consecutive unemployment.
His arguments are the current and the preceding year's unemployment rate and the proportion of workers 45 years of age and
over. (This older worker ratio is important since persons past
age 45 are most susceptible to long spells of joblessness.)
Simler's model indicates that changes in size of the unemployment stock are accompanied by disproportionate changes in long
duration unemployment. A sustained change of 1.0 percentage
point in the unemployment rate results in a 0.2 percentage
point change in long duration unemployment. Given the current
proportion of older workers, a steady state unemployment rate

---

[10]Assuming that each unemployed worker has an equal chance of
emerging from unemployment, 11 percent of unemployed white
males in December 1961 would have been unemployed for 15-26
weeks, and 3 percent for a longer period. See Barbara R.
Berman, "An Approach to an Absolute Measure of Structural Unemployment," in *Employment Policy and the Labor Market*, ed.,
Arthur M. Ross (Berkeley: University of California Press,
1965), p. 268.

of four percent is associated with long duration unemployment of 0.4.[11]

The Department of Labor also publishes annually reports on work experience during the prior year. These reports allow us to classify the long duration unemployed into two groups: those who experienced between 27 and 39 weeks of unemployment, and those who experienced 40 or more weeks of unemployment. Importantly, the statistics refer to the total number of workers who have experienced unemployment during the year rather than to annual averages, and classification is based on total rather than on consecutive weeks of unemployment. Total weeks may be the superior criteria since even a structurally unemployed worker may be able to secure employment for brief periods. An employer may overestimate his potential productivity and initiate a new hire, only to discover and correct the error during the probationary period. Alternatively, a worker's problem may be chronic rather than consistent inefficiency. For psychological and physical reasons, a worker's capacity for effective job performance may be limited to several weeks, ensuring that each job is a short one. A dual set of reservations is also possible. A worker may insist on an unrealistically high wage for a permanent job, but be willing to accept temporary jobs at lower wages. The major disadvantage of the work experience data is that spells of unemployment are not regularly cumulated beyond the calendar year.[12]

Among persons 18 years of age and over who performed some work during 1964, a year when the unemployment rate was 5.2 percent, 1.3 percent experienced unemployment of 27 to 39 weeks, and 0.6 percent experienced unemployment of 40 weeks or longer.

---

[11]"Long Term Unemployment, The Structural Hypothesis and Public Policy," *American Economic Review*, December 1964.

[12]Such cumulation is provided for the period 1960-62 for persons who were unemployed 5 weeks or more in 1962. Relevant results are shown below in summary form.

Employment Status in April 1963	Months of Unemployment, 1960-62			
	7 to 12	13 to 18	19 to 24	25 to 36
	(in 000's)			
Total	1,695	1,341	814	667
Labor Force	1,598	1,323	700	592
Employed	1,337	941	443	265
Unemployed	621	382	257	327
Not in Labor Force	97	18	114	75

Source: Carol B. Kalish, "A Portrait of the Unemployed," U.S. Department of Labor, Bureau of Labor Statistics, Special Labor Force Report No. 61, Table B.

The comparable figures for 1969, when the unemployment rate was 3.5 percent, were 0.6 and 0.3 percent. Most long duration unemployment is thus concentrated in the 27 to 39 week rather than in the open-ended 40 week and over category. Both categories benefit disproportionately when total unemployment falls.

On the basis of available data, structural unemployment seems to have affected considerably less than one percent, perhaps considerably less than one-half of one percent of the labor force. Structural unemployment is, of course, a highly restrictive concept. It is an incomplete measure of the hardships of the labor market adjustment process, since spells of frictional unemployment may be onerously long, and since some unknown number of workers who otherwise would be structurally unemployed ultimately abandon job search and disappear from the official statistics.

CONCLUSIONS

Unemployment has been classified into three mutually exclusive and exhaustive categories, frictional, demand deficiency, and structural.[13] All three categories are shown graphically

---

[13]This scheme emphasizes the reason for the persistence of the unemployment experience. Unemployment is traced to job search, job shortage, unrealistic reservations, or factor shortages. The approach is analytically appealing, since it calls attention to the processes that generate unemployment. An alternative approach classifies unemployment by the optimum policy response. Unemployment that would be removed by monetary or fiscal policy would be classified as demand deficiency, that to be treated by labor market policy as structural, and that to be endured as frictional unemployment. See Richard G. Lipsey, "Structural and Deficient-Demand Unemployment Reconsidered," in *Employment Policy and The Labor Market*, ed., Arthur M. Ross, pp. 210-216. Some comparison of the two approaches is desirable. We would classify unemployment arising from a short fall of aggregate demand as demand deficiency unemployment. Lipsey would reserve this classification for unemployment to be treated by monetary and fiscal policy. Suppose that inflation occurs before full employment is reached and that full reliance on monetary and fiscal policy is inhibited by an aversion to inflation. Some workers would then remain unemployed because of a shortage of jobs. Lipsey would classify these workers as frictionally unemployed, since society prefers the unemployment to the remedy (inflation). Such an approach seems to obscure rather than to illuminate problems and options. The choice between definitions is not solely a matter of taste. Some cast more light than others.

in Figure 6. The magnitude AC is frictional unemployment. The magnitude EA is demand deficiency unemployment. All persons located to the right of C on the S_{L+U} schedule, who appear in the official unemployment statistics, are structurally unemployed.

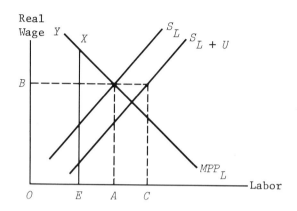

Figure 6. Types of Unemployment

Frictional unemployment is voluntary and compatible with full employment. It exists because workers search the labor market rather than accepting just any job offer. The likeliest instances of structural unemployment are also voluntary. They result from workers with unrealistic and irreducible reservations searching the labor market. Demand deficiency unemployment represents a departure from full employment and is involuntary. It is traceable to macroeconomic disorder rather than to worker behavior or labor market structure. Wage flexibility is theoretically capable of resolving demand deficiency unemployment through its financial and product market repercussions. As a practical matter, instituting new monetary and fiscal policies is the appropriate response to demand deficiency unemployment.

Waiving the inflation problem (to which we turn in the next chapter), full employment is clearly a desirable social objective. Few would quarrel with the assertion that jobs should be available for all those willing to work at a wage commensurate with their productivity. However, full employment is not the ultimate labor market objective. Considerable social and economic inequity can coexist with full employment.

Structural unemployment may be a problem of trivial magnitude, but it is not trivial to those afflicted by it. The human costs of free labor markets can be high. Social justice requires not only full employment, but also attention to the problems of the technically obsolete, the geographically stranded, the genetically underendowed, and the environmentally disadvantaged.

6

Unemployment Problems of the American Economy

This chapter surveys the unemployment problems and contro-
versies of the modern American economy. It does so by explor-
ing in detail three subjects: the characteristics of the unemployed, the unemployment record of the past quarter of a
century, and the unemployment-inflation dilemma.

Unemployment experiences are not equally distributed.
Some labor markets suffer very high unemployment even when the
overall economy is prosperous. Members of some groups are virtually immune to unemployment, while others are highly vulnerable. A Ph.D. biologist, psychologist, or economist who experiences any unemployment is a rarity. An urban laborer with an
eighth grade education or a black teenager who does not have a
number of unemployment experiences, some quite protracted, is
also a rarity. Why these differences? We will seek insight by
examining the incidence of unemployment during a full employment period and then during a period of demand deficiency. We
will be concerned with who experiences unemployment and why
some groups are so vulnerable.

INCIDENCE AT FULL EMPLOYMENT

The fact that different labor force subgroups have different frictional unemployment rates is the key to understanding
the incidence of unemployment at full employment.[1] Some workers have higher propensities to enter the labor market or to
quit jobs. Some have greater vulnerability to layoff. Some
are fussier about job requirements and hunt longer. Frictional
unemployment is not synonymous with low unemployment. Some
groups will have high frictional rates. For example, a quit-

---

[1]Melvin W. Reder, "The Theory of Frictional Unemployment,"
Economica, February 1969, pp. 1-28.

prone group whose members resigned their jobs every nine weeks
and spent a week hunting new employment would experience a
frictional rate of ten percent. The stability characteristics
of industries, occupations, and demographic groups vary sharply.
Consequently, some groups experience much while other groups
experience little frictional unemployment.

In 1969, the unemployment rate was 3.5 percent. Some of
this could have been structural, but the major component was
undoubtedly frictional. Unemployment in government, in finance,
and in professional services hovered around two percent. These
activities seldom engage in layoffs since output levels are
relatively stable from month to month. In contrast, the unemployment rate in construction was six percent. Construction is
a highly seasonal and irregular activity. Many on-site workers
are hired for particular jobs rather than as permanent employees. They are exposed to intermittent spells of unemployment as they move from job to job. In 1969, the unemployment
rate in retail trade was 4.1 percent. The volume of trade is
highly uneven, with peaks during the Christmas and Easter sea-
sons. In addition, retail trade employs a considerable number
of married women, some of whom fluctuate between nonlabor force
and labor force status, depending on the availability of job
opportunities, the needs of their families, and their inclinations of the moment. These women are exposed to the prospect
of unemployment each time they reenter the labor market. Thus,
the 1969 unemployment rate was 2.8 percent for men and 4.7 percent for women.

As discussed earlier, quit rates are low in activities
with high wages and attractive job ladders. Workers with desirable jobs are most likely to stay put. Looking at some of
the higher paying occupations, unemployment was 0.9 percent
among managers and officials, 1.3 percent among professional
and technical workers, and 2.2 percent among craftsmen and foremen. The unemployment rate was also low in industries that employ large numbers of manual workers, but pay high wages. Unemployment was 1.6 percent in railroads, 2.2 percent in primary
metals, and 2.8 percent in mining. In contrast, low wage activities lack holding power and frequently employ quit-prone
workers, who have difficulty meeting the high hiring standards
set for attractive jobs. Thus, the unemployment rate was 4.4
percent among operatives and 6.7 percent among nonfarm laborers.
Among the lower paying industries, it was 4.2 percent in tex-
tiles, 4.7 percent in nonprofessional services, and 6.0 percent
in apparel and among farm workers. These high unemployment
rates testify not to labor surplus but to labor turnover.

The unemployment experience of teenagers and Negroes de-
serves more extended analysis. Both groups suffer a host of
labor market problems and experience high unemployment. A variety of special explanations has been offered for this high

unemployment. The most frequently cited villain is the elimination of low skilled and "entry jobs" by automation. Negro unemployment is often traced to the influx of undereducated and
ill prepared Negroes to the central cities and the exodus of
more prosperous whites to the suburbs. These special explanations are not completely devoid of merit. Nonetheless, the
frictional model provides the major explanation of high teenage
and Negro unemployment.

Teenagers

In 1955, the teenage unemployment rate was 11.0 percent
and the adult rate 3.9 percent.[2] The labor market position of
younger workers deteriorated to the point where, in 1969, the
teenage rate was 12.2 percent while the adult rate was only 2.6
percent. The popular literature attributes this deterioration
to the elimination of the low skilled and semiskilled blue collar "entry jobs," through which teenagers traditionally acquired work experience and set a foot on the promotion ladder.[3]
The concept of entry jobs disappearing is, of course, untenable.
Every ladder must have a bottom rung. In every industry, there
are low echelon jobs for which novices are hired. The problem
has been not a dearth of jobs but a bulge in the teenage population. In 1947, persons 16 to 19 years of age accounted for
6.9 percent of total employment. The teenage population declined during most of the 1950s, and by 1958 teenagers filled
only 5.7 percent of all jobs. After that, teenage population
rose, and so did the teenage share of total jobs, reaching 7.8
percent by 1971. Between 1960 and 1971, teenage employment
rose by 2.1 million or 50 percent, while total employment was
increasing by 13.3 million or 20 percent. Clearly, teenage job
opportunities are not being eliminated. Teenage employment has
grown impressively, but not quite as impressively as has the
teenage population and labor force.
       The rise in school enrollment has aggravated the problem
of increased supply. The typical teenager is enrolled in
school. The competing claims on his time and energy generally
do not permit him to compete seriously for entry jobs on a promotion ladder. He is seeking part-year and part-time work that

---

[2]For a fuller discussion of teenage labor market problems and
prospects, see Edward Kalachek, *The Youth Labor Market*, Policy
Papers in Human Resources and Industrial Relations No. 12 (Ann
Arbor: Institute of Labor and Industrial Relations, The University of Michigan-Wayne State University, January 1969).

[3]A summary of the "entry job" argument is contained in Charles
Silberman, "What Hit the Teenagers," *Fortune*, April 1965.

will yield some income and some work experience. The standard
job is not appropriate to the needs of most teenagers. They
want weekend, after school, or summer jobs. The growing supply
of teenagers has resulted in longer job hunts and placed downward pressure on teenage wages. With some time lag, employers
have responded to the ready availability of occasional labor
and to the reduction of relative teenage wages. One aspect of
the response has been the growth of retail franchises that depend on part-time teenage workers for a considerable portion of
their work force.

In other words, the teenage labor market was disturbed
by a population bulge that shifted the supply schedule to the
right. The new equilibrium was approached gradually rather
than instantaneously. Time is required for employers to real-
ize their new opportunities and to adjust their production
processes and hiring procedures accordingly. This adjustment
process should soon be complete. The peak rate of growth in
teenage population has passed. In 1971, persons from ages 16
to 19 accounted for 10.5 percent of the noninstitutional population. In 1975, they will account for 10.7 percent, and in
1980, for 10.1 percent. The significant substitution of teenage for adult labor, which occurred during the 1960s, as the
teenage share of total employment rose from 5.7 to 7.8 percent,
will not be necessary in the future.

In the new equilibrium, teenage unemployment will be substantially higher than adult unemployment, as it was even before the population bulge occurred. High teenage unemployment
is primarily voluntary. A Bureau of Labor Statistics tabula-
tion of the channels through which unemployment was entered
during six selected months of 1964-66 indicates why high teenage rates can be expected.[4] The unemployment rate for these
months was 5.1 percent for all workers and 16.4 percent for
teenagers. Labor market entrance and reentrance accounted for
a teenage unemployment rate of 13.1 percent and for an overall
rate of 2.5 percent. If we eliminate this origin of joblessness, the teenage unemployment rate falls to 3.3 percent, and
the overall rate to 2.6 percent. Teenagers will normally be
unemployed more frequently than adults simply because their in-
volvement in school activities results in a high rate of labor
force entrance and reentrance.

---

[4]Kathryn D. Hoyle, "Why the Unemployed Look for Work," U.S.
Department of Labor, Bureau of Labor Statistics, Special Labor
Force Report No. 78, p. 35.

Negroes

In 1969, the unemployment rate was 3.1 percent for whites
and 6.3 percent for Negroes and other races. Why the adverse
Negro experience? Some have pointed to the growing polariza-
tion of the central city and the suburbs. They argue that blue
collar and low skilled jobs are increasingly located in the suburbs. Less skilled Negroes generally live in the central
cities. The suburbanization of industry is thus lengthening
their journey to work. This can be a severe problem for those
workers lacking automobiles, since public transit does not adequately service suburban work sites. Low skilled white workers
can solve the problem by moving closer to suburban work sites
or to transit lines that connect them with the work sites.
This option is frequently foreclosed to Negroes by housing segregation. Consequently, they find it difficult or impossible
to get jobs available in distant suburbs.[5] Unemployment in the
central cities coexists with labor shortage in the suburbs.

This transportation deficiency argument, although plausi-
ble, seems grossly overdrawn. It explains some Negro teenage
unemployment, though. Housing segregation and poor public
transportation separate Negro teenagers from the middle and
upper income families and the myriad of retail establishments
that offer part-time jobs. However, adults are another matter.
For them, the central city remains the major job center. It
still has the largest concentration of low and medium skilled
jobs. Despite the suburbanization of industry, the net flow of
low and medium skilled commuters is still toward, rather than
away from, the central city. Government subsidized experimen-
tal bus lines designed to link the ghetto unemployed with suburban work sites have generally had unimpressive records.
Neither employers nor the ghetto unemployed have been very interested. Why travel an hour on a bus to get an unskilled or
semiskilled job when similar jobs are readily available closer
to home?[6]

Automation notwithstanding, the demand for low skilled
workers is adequate during full employment periods. The Negro
unemployment problem is not structural but frictional; most
find jobs easily during high employment periods. Keeping a job
for any period of time is a different matter, and frequently

---

[5]See John F. Kain, "Housing Segregation, Negro Employment, and
Metropolitan Decentralization," *Quarterly Journal of Economics*,
May 1968; and Joseph Mooney, "Housing Segregation, Negro Employment, and Metropolitan Decentralization," *Quarterly Journal
of Economics*, May 1969.

[6]Edward D. Kalachek and John M. Goering, eds., *Transportation
and Central City Unemployment*, pp. 1-18.

far more difficult.[7] Young Negroes and those without dependents have extremely high job turnover rates, sometimes treating
jobs as temporary sources of income only, often moving from one
unsatisfactory position to another. Is this job instability
the result of a distinctive ghetto value system that manifests
and propagates disorganized values and motivations? Or, are
the racial designations *white* and *Negro* simply proxies for the
familiar high wage/low quit rate and low wage/high quit rate
relationships? The answer is still unclear, although personality surveys indicate that ghetto values are compatible with
demands for individual achievement and industrial discipline.

> The high quit rates of young Negroes appear due
> not to a deviant value system but to the frustration
> of low paying jobs. . . . Younger workers appear less
> willing or able to accept poverty level wages when
> they perceive the value system of the "American Dream"
> to be promising more. To solve the Negro unemploy-
> ment problem we must either learn how to teach the
> young Negro to modify his high expectations or else
> we must significantly alter conditions limiting his
> productivity.[8]

Unfortunately, antipoverty programs have operated until
recently on the assumption that the problem of lower skilled
workers, Negro or otherwise, was finding a job. The real problem is finding a job sufficiently attractive to be worth keeping. Antipoverty programs in manpower should be redirected
toward sharply raising worker productivity and encouraging attitudes and habits conducive to lengthy job tenure.

INCIDENCE DURING DEMAND DEFICIENCY PERIODS

All unemployment rates rise in a consistent and highly predictable fashion when demand deficiency develops. However,
they do not rise equally. The uneven incidence characteristic
of full employment is further accentuated. The absolute value
of indices of the dispersion of unemployment by occupation almost doubles between the peak and trough years of a business
cycle. Demand deficiency has the sharpest impact on workers in
goods producing industries, in low skilled occupations, on

---

[7]Peter B. Doeringer, "Manpower Programs for Ghetto Labor Markets," in *Proceedings of the 21st Annual Meeting Industrial Relations Research Association*, ed., Gerald Somers, pp. 257-267.

[8]Edward D. Kalachek and John M. Goering, eds., *Transportation
and Central City Unemployment*, p. 9.

Negroes, and on teenagers. An increase of one percentage point
in the experienced worker unemployment rate is associated with
an increase of 1.7 percentage points for durable goods manufacturing workers and miners, 1.9 percentage points for construction workers, 1.8 percentage points for semiskilled workers,
2.6 percentage points for unskilled workers, and 2 percentage
points for both Negroes and teenagers. Demand deficiency has
a more modest impact on workers in government, finance, and
service industries, and in white collar and high skill activities. When the experienced worker rate increases by one percentage point, unemployment rises by 0.3 percentage point for
finance and government workers, 0.6 percentage points for service industry workers, 0.25 percentage points for professional
and technical workers, 0.7 percentage points for clerical workers, and 1.3 percentage points for craftsmen.

Why these differences? Industrial differences reflect
varying sensitivity to cyclical fluctuations. Recessions have
their sharpest impact in the urban goods producing sector, and
their weakest impact in the government-finance-service sectors.
As the prospect of income becomes dim, consumers postpone their
plans to purchase new automobiles and household appliances.
Businesses reconsider or postpone investment expenditures and
deplete inventories. Construction business weakens as households postpone purchases of new homes and firms delay the purchase of new plants. Less factory output means less demand for
coal to stoke the furnaces. In contrast, the consumption of
services cannot be inventoried or as readily displaced.

Occupational differences are in part simply the result of
industrial differences. The unemployment of low and semiskilled blue collar workers is cyclically sensitive because
these workers are heavily concentrated in durable goods manufacturing, construction, and mining. The unemployment of professional and other highly skilled workers is less sensitive
because so many are employed by government and nonprofit institutions. In addition, employers in cyclically sensitive activities are reluctant to lay off highly skilled workers. They
may have invested heavily in their training and be earning a
rent on their employment. It may be less expensive to hoard
highly trained workers, allowing them to bump down into less
skilled categories, than to scramble to rehire them comes the
upturn. Even if he is laid off, the professional or highly
skilled worker has a higher probability of finding reemployment
rapidly than does his less skilled brethren. In a pinch, a
skilled worker can find employment as a semiskilled or unskilled worker. The unskilled worker has no such bumping down
options.[9]

---

[9]Melvin W. Reder, "The Theory of Occupational Wage Differences,"
American Economic Review, December 1955.

Teenagers are disproportionately affected by recessions because they are the most recent labor force entrants. Since they are most likely to be job hunters, they are most likely to be frozen out of jobs by a slackening or cessation of hiring. If they do have jobs, teenagers are low on the seniority list and vulnerable to layoff. Negroes are also highly vulnerable since they are heavily concentrated in low skilled and cyclically sensitive activities. Furthermore, when jobs are scarce, employers raise hiring standards and pick and choose among workers. A ready availability of labor makes it more possible for racial prejudice to enter into hiring and firing decisions.

During periods of economic slack, the unemployment stock is filled with the young, the low skilled, and the black—precisely those who elicit the least enthusiasm from employers. The unemployed seem unemployable. Politicians, journalists, and trade union leaders wonder whether these inadequately educated and low skilled workers can ever hope to find employment. After all, industry increasingly needs more highly trained white collar workers and fewer uneducated manual workers. Nonetheless, the unemployed still find jobs during cyclical recoveries, because hiring policies during such recoveries have little to do with long term employment trends.[10] Employers retain their supervisory, professional, technical, and skilled personnel during periods of slack. They do not need more such workers to expand output; instead, they need and rehire the low skilled blue collar workers previously laid off. The hiring policies of the recovery undo the damage of the firing policies of the recession.

THE RECORD

With the miseries of the Great Depression still strongly in mind, Congress passed the Employment Act of 1946. In somewhat guarded and qualified language, this act committed the federal government to an interventionist stance on unemployment:

> The Congress hereby declares that it is the continuing policy and responsibility of the Federal Government to use all practicable means consistent with its needs and obligations, and other essential considerations of national policy, with the assistance and cooperation of industry, agriculture, labor and state and local governments, to coordinate and utilize all

---

[10]Barbara A. Bergmann and David E. Kaun, *Structural Unemployment in The United States*, U.S. Department of Commerce (Washington, D.C.: U.S. Government Printing Office, 1966), Chapter III.

its plans, functions and resources for the purpose of
creating and maintaining, in a manner calculated to
foster and promote the general welfare, conditions
under which there will be afforded useful employment
opportunities, including self-employment for those
able, willing and seeking to work, and to promote
maximum employment, production and purchasing power.[11]

During the quarter of a century since then, the unemployment rate has averaged 4.7 percent, a favorable performance by
historical standards.[12] The 4.7 percent is an average of good
and moderately bad years. Unemployment has fluctuated widely
in response to differential growth rates in aggregate demand
and supply. During the postwar reconversion boom of 1947-48,
unemployment averaged 3.9 percent. The boom terminated and in
the 1949-50 recession, unemployment averaged 5.6 percent. Recovery occurred rapidly. The military requirements of the Korean War were superimposed on already strong civilian demands
for goods and services, and the draft restricted the growth of
the civilian labor force. The unemployment rate averaged an
extremely low 3.1 percent during 1951-53. The end of the war
and the ensuing reduction of federal expenditures precipitated
the mild recession of 1954. Unemployment rose to 5.5 percent.
However, latent private demands remained strong. Due to the
dearth of consumer and business investments during the depression and the Second World War, household stocks of consumer
durables and business stocks of plant and equipment were considerably less than desired, given the community's income and
liquidity.
    The 1954 recession was succeeded by the investment boom of
1955-57, during which unemployment averaged 4.3 percent.
Events then took a turn for the worse. Unemployment averaged
6.8 percent during the severe 1958 recession. It hovered
around 5.5 percent during the mild and short-lived recovery of

[11]*Employment Act of 1946, as Amended, with Related Laws*, 90th
Congress, 1st Session (Washington, D.C.: U.S. Government Printing Office, 1967), p. 1.

[12]Unemployment averaged 8.0 percent during the first 40 years
of this century. This average falls to 4.6 percent if the depression decade of the 1930s is excluded. However, it should
not be excluded from this comparison since the great accomplish-
ment of post World War II economic planning has been the avoid-
ance of such protracted mass joblessness. See Stanley Leber-
gott, "Annual Estimates of Unemployment in the United States,
1900-1954," in *The Measurement and Behavior of Unemployment*,
National Bureau of Economic Research (Princeton, New Jersey:
Princeton University Press, 1957), pp. 205-216.

1959-60, rose to 6.7 percent during the 1961 recession, and fell to 5.6 percent during the recovery and expansion of 1962-63. The percent to which unemployment fell during recoveries was now the same as the percent to which it rose during the recessions of 1949-50 and 1954. The unemployment ceiling of recessions had been converted into the unemployment floor of recoveries. This was a disturbing matter.

The Demand Deficiency-Structural Change Debate

A great public debate ensued on the causes of higher unemployment and on the appropriate remedies. The President's Council of Economic Advisers used Keynesian income analysis to interpret the post 1957 deterioration. The Council attributed higher unemployment to a deficiency of aggregate demand. Ex ante savings and tax receipts had grown more rapidly than ex ante investment and government expenditures at full employment. Government expenditures and tax rates were generating a full employment budget surplus. Consequently, full employment could be attained only if ex ante private investment substantially exceeded ex ante savings. After 1957, private investment was no longer sufficiently buoyant. Aggressive monetary and fiscal measures were needed to stimulate demand.[13] On the other hand, the Board of Governors of the Federal Reserve System and many others attributed the higher unemployment largely to technical changes that were transforming the structure of the American economy. The problem was not a shortage of jobs but a mismatch of jobs and workers. The unemployment rate associated with full employment had risen. The appropriate remedy was labor market policy. Retraining could provide workers with skills currently in demand. Monetary and fiscal stimulation would simply increase the demand for highly educated and trained workers, already in short supply, and lead to inflation.[14]

---

[13]See, for instance, *The Annual Report of the Council of Economic Advisers* in *Economic Report of the President* (Washington, D.C.: U.S. Government Printing Office, January 1962), Chapter 1.

[14]See, for instance, "Statement of William McChesney Martin, Jr., Chairman, Board of Governors of the Federal Reserve System" and subsequent questioning and submissions in *U.S. Congress, January 1961 Economic Report of the President and the Economic Situation and Outlook, Hearings before the Joint Economic Committee*, 87th Congress, 1st Session (Washington, D.C.: U.S. Government Printing Office, 1961), pp. 462-501; and Congressman Tom Curtis, *87 Million Jobs, A Dynamic Program to End Unemployment* (New York: Duell, Sloan and Pearce, 1962).

Everyone agreed that technical change was reshaping the
economy. The occupational composition of the labor force had
been changing dramatically for some time, as shown in Table 2.
During the first five decades of this century, the significant
changes were the urbanization of the labor force, the growth of
white collar activities, and the decline, first relative and
then absolute, in the demand for unskilled labor. The employment of manual and especially of semiskilled (operative) workers in manufacturing and other urban goods producing activities
grew rapidly during this period. The continuing transformation
of the labor force showed some striking new twists during the
1950s. Urban blue collar and manufacturing employment peaked
in 1953, and a decade later were still below that peak. The
locus of growth in white collar employment passed from the
clerical and sales to the professional and technical occupations. White collar jobs were now requiring advanced educational attainment. These new developments seemed related to
automation.

Everyone agreed on the facts but differed in their inter-
pretations. The aggregate demand theorists considered employers and workers flexible enough to accommodate to these changes.
The structural transformation theorists saw inflexibilities,
mismatching, and an aggravation of frictional and structural
unemployment. They argued that technical change had led traditionally to the specialization of function and to the division
of the production process into a large number of simplified operations that could be performed by workers of moderate skill
and capability. The 1950s and 1960s were, however, marked by
the development and rapid introduction of increasingly advanced
computers, feedback mechanisms, and automatic sensory instruments, and by the occasional integration of these systems in a
single, fully automated production unit. This tendency of automation to reintegrate the production process sharply reduced
the demand for semiskilled assembly line workers while increasing the demand for highly skilled maintenance men, responsible
machine tenders, and other educated, sophisticated, and flexible workers. Blue collar workers, laid off from industrial employment, found their skills obsolete, their education deficient, and found that they frequently lacked the personality
requisite to finding jobs in the rapidly growing finance, trade,
service, and government sectors. Automation had created an imbalance between the skills and attainments of unemployed workers and the requirements of the new jobs.

Given two alternative hypotheses, social scientists devise
tests to select the more correct alternative. Politicians are
possessed of a different wisdom: they are more inclined to compromise differences than to choose between hypotheses. Congress legislated the policies proposed by both parties to the
dispute (between the aggregate demand theorists and the struc-

Table 2. Decade-to-Decade Change in Labor Force by Major
Occupation Group (Percent Change)*

Major Occupation Group	1960 to 1970	1950 to 1960	1940 to 1950	1930 to 1940	1920 to 1930	1910 to 1920	1900 to 1910
Total	19	11	14	6	15	13	28
White Collar Workers	34	28	34	12	36	32	56
Professional, technical and kindred workers	50	65	31	17	45	30	42
Managers, officials and proprietors, except farm	17	9	37	4	29	14	45
Clerical and kindred workers	41	28	45	15	28	70	127
Sales workers	15	13	20	13	49	17	34
Manual Workers	14	5	18	7	14	19	37
Craftsmen, foremen and kindred workers	12	12	35	-1	14	27	41
Operatives and kindred workers	15	0	26	24	17	21	46
Laborers, except farm and mine	1	6	-20	-9	9	10	24
Service Workers	20	26	2	27	44	-7	36
Private household workers	-22	16	-36	21	42	-24	17
Service workers, except private household workers	34	31	27	32	46	11	63
Farm Workers	-40	-26	-23	-13	-9	-1	6
Farmers and farm managers	-37	-36	-18	-11	-6	5	7
Farm laborers and foremen	-43	-12	-29	-15	-13	-8	5
Farm and nonfarm laborers	-16	-2	-24	-12	-2	1	13

*Percentage changes pertain to the economically active civilian
population for the period 1900 to 1950 and to the civilian labor force for the period 1950-1970.

Source: U.S. Department of Commerce, Bureau of the Census, Working Paper No. 5, "Occupational Trends in the United States 1900-
1950," various issues of *The Monthly Report on the Labor Force*,
and *Manpower Report of the President, April 1971.*

tural transformation theorists). Congress enacted an 11 billion dollar reduction in tax rates in early 1964, with the intent of greatly stimulating aggregate demand. A wide range of
labor market policies were also adopted during the 1960s, first
in response to the fears of structural unemployment, and later
as part of the antipoverty program. Unemployment soon began
to fall, ushering in a protracted period of tight labor markets.
The unemployment rate averaged 5.2 percent in 1964, 4.5 percent
in 1965, 3.8 percent in 1966, and reached a low of 3.5 percent
in 1969. The investment in labor market policy was not sufficient to explain this marked improvement. Expenditures on the
new manpower programs rose from only 60 million dollars in fiscal 1963 to about two-thirds of a billion dollars in fiscal
1966. The unprecedentedly long prosperity of the 1960s was undoubtedly traceable to the stimulation of aggregate demand. By
itself, the 1964 tax cut would probably have left unemployment
somewhere above four percent. However, the Vietnam War en-
larged; the expenditures it commanded were not fully offset by
the temporary tax increase of 1968, nor by stringency in other
government programs. Both the tax reduction and the unexpected
expenditure demands of the Vietnam War stimulated a major investment boom and drove unemployment below four percent.

The industrial, occupational, racial, and age pattern of
the decline in unemployment, which occurred after early 1964,
was typical for cyclical recoveries and expansions. Declines
were sharpest among urban goods producing workers, low skilled
blue collar workers, Negroes, and teenagers. In retrospect,
the high unemployment experienced by these groups in 1958-63
was not symptomatic of any new structural problem. Rather, it
was the normal concomitant of deficient demand and loose labor
markets.

Labor Market Policy

The labor market policies adopted during the 1960s, though
modest in size, represent important innovations and the larger
of them merit some mention.[15] The most important was the Manpower Development and Training Act (MDTA), originally passed in
1962, and subsequently amended in a number of important ways.
MDTA is aimed at the disadvantaged, the low skilled, and the
obsolete worker. It seeks to raise their productivity and em-
ployability. MDTA supports institutional programs in which

---

[15]The rich set of current labor market policies is described
and analyzed in Sar A. Levitan and Garth L. Mangum, *Federal
Training and Work Programs in the Sixties* (Ann Arbor: Institute
of Labor and Industrial Relations, 1969).

workers (who receive subsistence allowances) are instructed and counselled in essentially schoollike settings. It also subsidizes on-the-job training programs (OJT) conducted by private firms. The program originally emphasized institutional training that would provide useful skills for a variety of jobs. Some years of experience led to disenchantment. Institutional training did not appear sufficiently oriented to skills currently in demand. In theory, OJT provided narrower and less versatile training, but it also provided a surer path to employment. Experience also demonstrated the critical importance of high job turnover propensities. Training and counselling conducted by the employer seemed more likely to encourage job stability than training conducted under institutional auspices. Consequently, the lion's share of manpower training funds are now allocated for training at the work site.

The Neighborhood Youth Corps was instituted to cope with high school dropout rates among disadvantaged youth and high teenage unemployment. It provides part-time jobs, work experience, and income for school attenders, a full-time work program for out-of-school youth, ages 16 to 20, and summer work programs. Politically popular, the Neighborhood Youth Corps has remained controversial among technical analysts. Although some regard it as an imaginative effort to ease the transition from school to work, others feel that it has only a marginal impact on skills and work discipline, and is really an effort to buy peace on ghetto streets. The belief that adverse family and community background was as serious a deterrent to effective labor market activity as lack of skills led to the creation of the Job Corps. The Job Corps provides general and vocational education and work experience in urban and rural residential centers. Despite its seemingly imaginative approach, the Job Corps was never overly popular with host communities. Its lack of community support, together with mediocre showings in cost-benefit studies, has led to its curtailment.

THE UNEMPLOYMENT-INFLATION DILEMMA

The low unemployment experienced during 1964-69 demonstrated the government's ability to generate and maintain tight labor markets. However, the ointment did not lack a fly. Low unemployment was accompanied by significant and accelerating price increases. Consumer prices rose by 1.7 percent in 1965, 2.9 percent in 1966, 2.9 percent in 1967, 4.2 percent in 1968, and 5.4 percent in 1969. Public distress at these price increases changed policy priorities. The antipathy to inflation led to increasingly stringent monetary and fiscal policies. The result was a retardation of economic growth and a shallow

recession. Unemployment began to rise in 1969, reached 4.9
percent in 1970, and 5.9 percent in 1971. This weakening of
demand only moderately retarded the onward rush of wages and
prices. The great prosperity of the 1960s had bred strong and
persisting inflationary expectations and pressures. Consumer
prices rose by 4.4 percent during the 12 months ending August
1971. The administration now desired to end the recession,
but it had not yet adequately coped with the inflation. The
stimulation of aggregate demand was politically feasible only
if inflation could be curbed. The administration broke with
peacetime precedent and in August 1971, instituted a three
month wage-price freeze, followed by an indefinite period of
wage and price controls.

The Kennedy-Johnson administration defended the 1964 tax
reduction by asserting that full employment could be achieved
without inflation. The Nixon administration defended the 1969-
70 curtailment of demand by asserting that price stability
could be achieved without a permanent increase in unemployment.
Both assertions imply that the level of unemployment and the
rate of change of money wages and prices lead independent lives.
Although both administrations said it, neither acted as though
they believed it. The Kennedy administration announced wage-
price guideposts and the Nixon administration wage-price controls in an effort to make low unemployment compatible with
stable prices. Are they compatible or is there a tradeoff?
Can we obtain low unemployment only by accepting inflation, and
price stability only by accepting high unemployment? This is
the key question confronting modern employment policy.

The Frictional Unemployment-Inflation Tradeoff

Assume that the economy is at full employment. The monetary and fiscal authorities misgauge the situation and stimulate aggregate demand by five percent. As shown in Figure 3,
additional workers will accept jobs only at higher real wages.
Employers will hire additional workers only at lower real wages.
Since monetary and fiscal stimulation shift neither the demand
nor the supply schedule, permanent employment gains are not
possible. Aggregate demand stimulation beyond full employment,
if correctly perceived, should result merely in a proportional
markup of wages and prices. Will correct perception occur immediately? We recall Alchian's dictum that aggregate demand
changes confuse market participants.[16]

[16]Armen A. Alchian, "Information Costs, Pricing and Resource
Unemployment," in *Microeconomic Foundations of Employment and
Inflation Theory*, eds., Edmund S. Phelps et al. (New York:
W. W. Norton and Company, Inc.), p. 42.

Assume that the behavior of the representative unemployed worker is adequately portrayed by the neoclassical theory of job search. Table 3 describes the relationship between acceptance wage and expected unemployment duration as perceived by this worker. On the basis of this perception, the direct costs of search, time preference, liquidity, and anticipated job tenure, the worker chooses a $3.00 acceptance wage and reconciles himself to an expected job hunt of five weeks. Table 3 is based on past labor market perceptions. Alchian's "confused worker" does not realize that all wages and prices are rising by five percent. He congratulates himself on a lucky break and accepts a $3.00 an hour job after four weeks of hunting. He has been fooled, since his objectives require a $3.15 an hour offer. A $3.00 an hour job now represents the same inferior position in the wage hierarchy and provides the same inferior purchasing power as a $2.85 an hour job did formerly. The worker obtained a job after four rather than five weeks of search because he accepted an inferior offer. The monetary and fiscal authorities have reduced the duration of unemployment and the frictional rate by deceiving the representative worker. They could have reduced unemployment even more by stage managing a larger wage and price increase.

The relationship between frictional unemployment and inflation is graphically portrayed in Figure 7. The time rate of change of money wages is plotted on the vertical axis. Unemployment is plotted on the horizontal axis. At OF all unemployment is frictional. It is assumed that full employment is consistent with zero wage change so long as workers anticipate a stable wage level. Unanticipated wage changes and the resulting unemployment levels trace out the P_1 schedule, a member of the family of schedules known as *Phillips curves*. The Phillips curve indicates that unemployment can be driven below its frictional level if we are willing to endure wage (and price) increases. Of course, a one period burst of wage (and price) increases will drive unemployment below its frictional level for

Table 3.   Hypothetical Demand Schedule Parameters for a Representative Unemployed Worker

Acceptance Wage	Expected Duration of Unemployment (Weeks)
$3.30	15
3.15	8
3.00	5
2.85	4
2.70	3
2.60	2
2.50	0

only that period. If wages and prices then stabilize, unemployment will return to OF.[17] If the monetary and fiscal authorities choose OD (in Figure 7) as their permanent unemployment target, they must increase demand sufficiently to raise
money wages by five percent each period. Such a policy can
achieve only temporary success.

The Phillips curve generated by deception is fragile. To
say that workers are confused by changes in aggregate demand is
to say that they are confused by unexpected and irregular
changes. A five percent increase in money wages, repeated period after period, will eventually become incorporated into the
expectations pattern of the dullest and most unperceptive worker. A worker hunting in period t for a job paying the equivalent of $3.00 an hour, defined in terms of period $t - 1$ rela-
tionships, will eventually learn that he must insist on $3.15
an hour. In graphic terms, the Phillips curve shifts to the
right, say from P_1 to P_2. Once workers learn the game, a five
percent rate of wage increase leaves unemployment at the frictional level of OF. A larger wage increase is now required to
reduce unemployment to OD. Repeated time after time, the
larger increase also becomes familiar, leading to yet another
Phillips curve shift. P_1 and P_2 are short-run schedules. The
long-run Phillips curve is perpendicular to the horizontal axis
at OF, the natural rate of unemployment.[18] The tradeoff between frictional unemployment and inflation is temporary, not
permanent.[19]

---

[17]Indeed, unemployment may rise above OF for a short period.
Deceived workers may find it advantageous to quit their jobs
and hunt for $3.15 an hour offers.

[18]See among others, Milton Friedman, "The Role of Monetary Policy," *American Economic Review*, March 1968, pp. 1-17, and the
already cited articles by Melvin Reder in *Economica*, and by
Armen A. Alchian, Donald F. Gordon and Allen Hynes, in *Microeconomic Foundations of Employment and Inflation Theory*. For a
dissenting view, see Albert Rees, "The Phillips Curve as a Menu
for Policy Choice," *Economica*, August 1970, pp. 227-238.

[19]A tradeoff is not to be disparaged simply because it is temporary. A one shot burst of unanticipated inflation may be the
most efficient means of handling a temporary rise in the natural rate, resulting from factor biased technical change. There
is also the important question of how temporary is temporary.
If workers learn slowly, the authorities may be able to hold
unemployment below its frictional level for lengthy periods.
It would be surprising, however, if workers did not perceive
the presence of inflation rapidly.

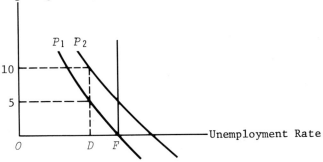

Figure 7.   The Phillips Curve

The deception theory provides a brilliant and compelling explanation of how excess demand can temporarily drive unemployment below its frictional level.   The brilliance and the pertinence of a theory are different matters, however.   Is the theory of worker deception pertinent to the American experience of the past quarter of a century?   Table 4 shows that prices increase substantially whenever the unemployment rate hovers at or below the four percent level.   In contrast, periods of higher unemployment are typified by relatively modest price advances.   The 1970-71 period is the major exception to the pairing of high unemployment with modest price increases.   It is not a devastating exception, since inflationary expectations linger on after their causes have evaporated.   Many wage increases result from long-term contracts negotiated earlier.   Cost increases work their way through the system with some lag.   The price increases of 1970-71 can legitimately be attributed to the preceding prosperity.   Likewise, the substantial 1958 price increase partially reflects the lagged impact of the 1955-57 expansion.   The 1949-50 data are distorted by an expectational rise in prices following the outbreak of the Korean War.

A strong inverse relationship exists between unemployment and inflation.   Prices rise rapidly at unemployment rates of four percent or less.   They are considerably more stable, though not perfectly so, at 5.5 percent unemployment.   This behavior is easily rationalized if full employment occurs at 5.5 percent or some higher rate.   Prices are relatively stable at 5.5 percent because supply and demand are fairly evenly balanced.   Prices rise sharply at four percent because of substantial excess demand.   Policy makers prove unwilling to tolerate the accelerating inflation required to maintain unemployment below the natural rate.   After interludes of four percent, they always switch their goals from low unemployment to stable prices.

Table 4.   Unemployment and Inflation*

Period	Unemployment Rate (Percent)	Consumer Price Index (Percentage Change)
Low Unemployment Periods		
1947–48	3.9	5.8
1951–53	3.1	2.5
1955–57	4.3	2.1
1964–69	4.1	3.4
High Unemployment Periods		
1949–50	5.6	2.0
1954	5.5	-.4
1958	6.8	1.7
1959–60	5.5	1.5
1961	6.7	.6
1962–63	5.6	1.5
1970–71	5.4	4.8

*Unemployment rates are averages for the specified periods. Changes in the Consumer Price Index (CPI) are average annual rates of change from the initial to the terminal December. For example, the 1947–48 change in the CPI is the average annual rate of change between December 1946 and December 1948.

Source: *Economic Report of the President, January 1972*, Tables B-2 and B-45, and various issues of the *Monthly Labor Review*.

Unfortunately, we must abandon easy rationalizations. It is too difficult to accept a 5.5 percent or higher rate as being full employment. Surely, vacant office buildings and closed factories are not the hallmark of full employment. In James Tobin's language, it "strains credulity." The behavior of quits, layoffs, average hours; the duration of unemployment, vacancies, investments in plant and equipment, profits, and capacity utilization rates all point to excess supply at 5.5 percent. President Kennedy's Council of Economic Advisers made a more reasonable assessment when they estimated that full employment occurred in the neighborhood of four percent. We conclude that the deception theory does not explain much of the inflationary experience of the American economy. Inflation has occurred mainly during periods of full employment or deficient demand.

The Demand Deficiency Unemployment-Inflation Tradeoff

Can inflation occur in the absence of excess demand? According to demand shift and cost-push theorists it can. Demand shift theorists perceive the economy as a composite of separate and heterogeneous labor and product markets that are loosely interrelated. National wage-unemployment trends are an aggregation of events occurring in the separate markets. Through time, the economy is continuously afflicted with technical advances, taste changes, and other disturbances. The irregular nature of these disturbances assures perpetual sectoral disequilibrium. There will always be some markets with excess demand and others with excess supply. Individual markets will vary irregularly between the two poles. Full employment for the economy does not imply full employment in each of the economy's markets. It simply implies a perfect balance between excess demand and excess supply markets. Now comes the crucial (though reasonable) assumption that wages rise more rapidly in response to excess demand than they fall in response to excess supply. If the assumption is correct, aggregate wages will rise at full employment. The nonlinearity of wage response gives the system a bias toward rising wages.[20] Wage stability requires some demand deficiency. A Phillips curve having nothing to do with worker deception or money illusion thus exists outside the frictional zone.[21]

---

[20]James Tobin, "Inflation and Unemployment," *American Economic Review*, March 1972, pp. 1-18.

[21]The demand shift theory assumes a dynamic economy. In such an economy, productivity is continuously increasing. The Phillips curve generated by demand shift will impart an

Cost-push theorists frequently consider collective bargaining the cause of inflation. The ability of trade unions to secure wage gains in excess of those generated by a free market
depends on their relative bargaining power. Companies will ac-
cede to terms favorable to the union when it is more costly to
fight than to settle. The agreement will be closer to manage-
ments' desires when the cost of intransigence falls most heavily on the union. The relative bargaining power of the union—
its relative ability to punish its bargaining adversary—varies
over the business cycle.

Union power is minimal when unemployment is high. Many
union members will have recently experienced unemployment or
short work weeks and will have neither the liquidity nor the
heart for a protracted strike. The union treasury will not be
buoyant since unemployed members frequently do not pay dues.
Workers often finance a strike by obtaining part-time or temporary jobs. High unemployment forecloses this option. Consequently, a long strike will induce liquidity crises in many
households.

If workers are vulnerable, employers are less so. A
strike can be costly to a company in at least three important
ways: (1) The company is deprived of profits from current operations. (2) If its customers cannot be serviced, they may
turn to alternative supply sources and find them attractive.
The company's long term market share and profit position is
thus threatened. (3) Skilled workers may take jobs elsewhere
if a strike drags on. This forces the company to additional
recruitment and training expenses in the post strike period.
These costs are all greatly mitigated when unemployment is
high. Profits and capacity utilization rates are likely to be
low. A plant closedown costs less when profits are low than
when they are high. Low capacity utilization rates allow goods
producing companies to recall laid off workers to produce for
inventory. If a strike is then called, inventories exist with
which to service customers. Production has been rearranged in
time. This rearrangement enables the company to weather a protracted strike with minimal costs, while liquidity pressures
mount on the high seniority workers who did not receive any
additional employment during the pre-strike period. The danger
of skilled workers going elsewhere is limited since there are
few elsewheres to go. An occasional illiquid firm will find a
recession a difficult time for collective bargaining, since any
interference with its flow of revenues may threaten bankruptcy.
Most firms, however, will find their favorable bargaining position in relation to the union one of the few redeeming aspects
of bad times.

---

[21]cont. inflationary bias only if wage gains at full employment exceed productivity gains.

As the economy moves closer to full employment, fewer union members will have recently experienced unemployment and short work weeks. Steady work will have reinvigorated their fighting spirit. Opportunities for finding auxiliary employment will be greater. Since plants will be operating closer to capacity, strikes will result in larger losses of output and profits. The losses may be real and permanent, since opportunities for inventory accumulation will be limited. The union's bargaining power is aggrandized. Enduring a protracted strike during a prosperity period is an expensive matter for employers. Settling on union terms is also expensive. Wage increases in excess of productivity advances lead to increases in marginal costs and prices. As relative prices rise, quantity sold declines. The consumer pays for part of the settlement by higher prices, but the company pays for part by lower profits.

Pattern bargaining—the tendency for one union to emulate the settlement of another—may substantially reduce the costs of settlement to the firm during prosperity periods and weaken its willingness to contest the union. Annual wage changes are highly similar in size, particularly in durable goods manufacturing industries.[22] Wage settlements in such industries as steel and autos are highly visible and widely publicized. The United Auto Workers and the United Steel Workers have organized plants in a number of industries. Members in these other industries expect gains commensurate with those achieved in autos and steel. Members of other unions, located in the same industrial centers and with similar levels of skill, may judge the quality of their leadership by its ability to match or surpass the auto and steel settlements. The result is pattern bargaining. Wage changes are linked together by what the late A. M. Ross felicitously called "orbits of coercive comparison." The organizing ability of a union, its leader's prestige, indeed his hold on power may depend on the rankings emerging from these invidious comparisons.[23]

The extent of pattern bargaining should not be exaggerated. Auto wage settlements will not permanently establish a pattern for the plastics industry if supply-demand conditions in the two industries diverge drastically. Neither should the impor-

---

[22]There are reasons besides pattern bargaining for the similarity of annual wage changes in durable goods industries. These industries draw on interrelated labor markets. They are all cyclically sensitive and are highly related on the demand side and in an input-output sense. A good year for consumer durables or capital equipment will result in a good year for their supplier industries.

[23]Arthur M. Ross, *Trade Union Wage Policy* (Berkeley: University of California Press, 1958).

tance of pattern bargaining be minimized; there is ample evidence of its existence.[24]

Pattern bargaining sharply reduces the cost of large wage settlements during prosperity periods. Given productivity gains, a three percent wage increase in steel may be compatible with stable marginal costs. However, the union will strike unless it receives six percent. A strike will be costly to the company. Settlement on union terms may not be as costly if other industries follow the pattern. A steel company executive agreeing to a six percent wage settlement may expect his action to shape behavior elsewhere. Unions in similar activities will be under pressure from their members to strike rather than to accept less. Company bargaining committees, if they agree to six percent, can report to their board of directors that they did no worse than steel. The directors may regard this as par for the course and prefer it to the long strike necessary to achieve a smaller settlement.[25] If other industries follow the steel pattern, they will experience similar cost increases and will mark up prices accordingly. Hence steel will suffer little or no relative price disadvantage (except in imports).

If aggregate monetary demand remains unchanged, the real demand for all goods and services, including steel, will decline. The resulting drop in output, profits, and employment will discipline all concerned parties and suggest the advisability of more moderate behavior in the future. However, this discipline will not be forthcoming if the monetary and fiscal authorities are sufficiently wedded to the goal of full employment. They will respond to deficient real demand by stimulating the economy.[26] This stimulation will permit continued high employment in the union sector, and lead to excess demand in the nonunion sector and a bidding up of wages and prices there. In the end, nobody will have gained much in real income; yet, nobody will have lost much. The large manufacturing corporations will have averted strikes and in the process have set off an inflation.

A Phillips curve for the demand deficiency zone can easily be inferred here. When unemployment is high, firms possess considerable bargaining power and are uncertain whether large wage increases will be emulated. They insist on modest settle-

[24]Otto Eckstein and Thomas Wilson, "The Determination of Money Wages in American Industry," *Quarterly Journal of Economics*, August 1962.

[25]Melvin W. Reder, "The Theory of Union Wage Policy," *Review of Economics and Statistics*, February 1952.

[26]J. R. Hicks, "The Economic Foundations of Wage Policy," *Economic Journal*, September 1955.

ments. When unemployment is low, the cost of strikes and the probability of emulation are both higher. Consequently, large wage increases are granted. These wage increases could easily assume inflationary magnitude at or before full employment. This Phillips curve is likely to be unstable. The tradeoff will depend on recent history. For instance, trade union members will be aggrieved at having received little real benefit from a six percent wage increase. If times are good when the next contract period rolls around, union members will be intent on securing a larger gain.

Money wage gains in excess of productivity advances are primarily dissipated by price markups. Bargaining for large money wage increases is normally a meaningless and potentially explosive game. Should trade union leaders be interested in playing the game? The answer is "yes." Those who are first to negotiate large money wage increases may secure at least temporarily some real advantage, while everyone else must follow suit for defensive reasons. The typical union member may give his leader credit for money wage gains and assign the blame for price increases elsewhere. If union leaders receive accolades for sizeable money wage increases, regardless of the real consequences of the increases, they will strive for such gains.

CONCLUSIONS

Inflation is the necessary result of using aggregate demand to push unemployment below its natural rate. Such efforts are only temporarily successful. To maintain unemployment at less than frictional levels requires accelerating inflation and continuously deceiving workers. However, our inflations are not generally traceable to such misdirected efforts. Prices begin to rise while demand is still deficient. The economy appears to have an inflationary bias, caused by demand shifts and/ or collective bargaining. We stand in need of policies to remove the bias. Labor market policy would be the appropriate antidote if inflation were due to heterogeneous labor markets and demand shifts. However, our experience with labor market policy has not been sufficiently encouraging to suggest that larger doses would substantially reduce the inflationary bias. If collective bargaining were the inflationary villain, we could dismantle the large companies and the large unions. It is dubious whether this is either politically feasible or socially desirable. Wage-price controls will have undesirable allocative effects, and there is no reason to be optimistic over their efficacy, given the peacetime experience of Western Europe.

All problems are not solvable. We may have to live with an economy in which inflation sets in before full employment.

On the other hand, we may not. The relationship between unemployment and money wage change is still not well understood.
It remains a frontier of research and public policy. Keynesian
income theory and experience with monetary, fiscal, and labor
market policy have enabled us to cope successfully with many of
the grosser and more severe unemployment problems. We are left
with a subtle but major problem. Is it possible to maintain
both low unemployment and stable prices? And if so, how?

7

Technical Change and the Labor Market

Technical change can be defined as an improvement in the ability to satisfy human wants from a given set of real resources.[1] The development of a new good that satisfies some want better or more cheaply than that desire could be satisfied by the existing constellation of goods and services is a technical change. Producing a traditional good at a lower real resource cost is also a technical change. Virtually every facet of the functioning of modern labor markets is conditioned by technical change. It has been the catalyst for dramatic improvements in real wages and living standards, for marked advances in human health, and for the elimination of much human drudgery in the work place and at home. Less favorably, technical change has been a continuing source of job instability. It has affected the total number of available jobs, as well as their geographic, industrial, and occupational locations. The important and frequently misunderstood relationships between technical change, employment stability, and the level of unemployment constitute the central concern of this chapter.

TOTAL EMPLOYMENT

Whenever technical change increases potential output, actual output remaining constant, jobs are destroyed. The same level of output is now producible using fewer real resources. On the other hand, if actual output is stimulated more than potential output, jobs are created. Technical change creates, leaves unchanged, or destroys jobs depending on whether it

---

[1]This chapter draws much of its inspiration from the research underlying Richard R. Nelson, Merton J. Peck, and Edward D. Kalachek, *Technology, Economic Growth and Public Policy* (Washington, D.C.: The Brookings Institution, 1967).

129

stimulates aggregate demand more, the same, or less than potential output. Clearly, technical change can lead to demand deficiency unemployment. When treating demand deficiency, Keynesian economics has been a major labor saving innovation. It
has disassociated the cure for unemployment from the cause.
The proper policy response for all practical purposes is independent of the precise causes of the demand impediment. Demand
deficiency unemployment arising from technical change is indistinguishable from demand deficiency unemployment arising from
other sources. So long as unemployment results from a deficiency of demand, it is susceptible to treatment by monetary
and fiscal policy.

In contrast with this view, the well publicized Ad Hoc
Committee on the Triple Revolution asserts that twentieth-
century automation is an unprecedented development. The employment problems it will create cannot be handled by any known
means. As the committee sees it, we are entering a world in
which monetary and fiscal policy will be unable to assure sufficient jobs. Revolutionary policy experiments will be required—a massive expansion of the public sector, a drastic
shortening of the work week, permanent income payments to able-
bodied adults living in leisure, or a moratorium on technical
change itself.[2]

The likelihood of consumer satiation is the crux of the
difference here. If consumers are unsatiated, the Keynesian
arguments are fully applicable. But what if the new techniques
of production are capable of turning out so many goods and
services with so little labor, that we are unable to consume
all the bounty? What if, as income rises, consumer desires for
goods and services become so well satisfied that latent demands
are weak or nonexistent? Charles C. Killingsworth observes:

> Look across the whole range of consumer goods and
> you will see that our mass consumption society has
> done a highly effective job of supplying the wants of
> the great majority of consumers. About 99.5 percent
> of the homes that are wired for electricity have elec-
> tric refrigerators; 93 percent have television sets;
> 83 percent have electric washing machines and we have
> even more radios than homes. The only sharply rising
> sales curve in the consumer durables field today is
> that of the electric can opener industry. The elec-
> tric toothbrush and electric hairbrush industries are
> starting to grow rapidly too. But the growth of em-

---

[2]See Donald N. Michael, *Cybernation: The Silent Conquest* (Santa
Barbara, California: Center for the Study of Democratic Institutions, 1962).

ployment in these new "industries" will not offset
the decline in the older, larger consumer goods
industries.[3]

Table 5 portrays the problem for closed economies. It
shows the growth path of potential output and aggregate demand
at full employment in two hypothetical economies. Potential
output starts at the same level and grows at the same pace in
both economies. The reasonable assumptions of a constant in-
vestment-potential output ratio and of a constant government
expenditure-potential output ratio are also made for both economies. As potential output triples from 100 to 300, investment
also triples from 10 to 30, and government from 20 to 60. Consumption behavior distinguishes the two economies. The consumers of the unsatiated economy spend a constant proportion of
their rising incomes on goods and services. The consumers of

Table 5. Potential Output and Aggregate Demand:
Two Hypothetical Cases

Time Period	Potential Output	Aggregate Demand at Full Employment			
		Total	Consumption	Investment	Government
		Unsatiated Economy			
1	100	100	70	10	20
2	200	200	140	20	40
3	300	300	210	30	60
		Satiated Economy			
1	100	100	70	10	20
2	200	180	120	20	40
3	300	240	150	30	60

the satiated economy are more jaded with materialism and less
excited about the joys of goods and services. Their consumption rises with income, but not proportionally. The components
of demand are well balanced in the unsatiated economy. Aggregate demand is capable of growing at the same pace as potential
output.
    In contrast, there is severe maladjustment in the satiated
economy. Aggregate demand falls consistently short of potential

---

[3]"Automation, Jobs and Manpower: The Case for Structural Unemployment," in *The Manpower Revolution: Its Policy and Consequences*, ed., Garth L. Mangum (New York: Doubleday and Co.,
1965), p. 90.

output at full employment. The satiated economy would be stag-
nant, with slow growth and high unemployment. The effectiveness of generalized monetary and fiscal policy is muted in this
economy. Lower interest rates will encourage a larger capital
stock. However, since the ultimate purpose of investment
goods is the production of consumption goods, the investment-
potential output ratio can only be expected to increase moderately. A low and declining marginal propensity to consume
means progressively smaller consumption multipliers. The effect of tax cuts on output will thus also be modest. Reliance
on government expenditure could always assure full employment,
since their first influence on output is not adversely affected.
In a society with a declining marginal propensity to consume,
such reliance would lead to a vastly expanded government sector.
In Table 5, maintaining full employment in the satiated economy
requires the government share of final output to rise from 20
to 40 percent. The Ad Hoc Committee is correct in pointing to
the need for revolutionary structural changes.

Consumer satiation would certainly be a problem, but it is
not ours. The American economy may be affluent, but in 1970,
annual disposable income per capita was only $3400. Median
family income was slightly under $10,000. This permits an his-
torically unprecedented standard of living, but one that still
falls considerably short of the societal ideal. The continuing
strength of consumer demand is shown by the fact that, in recent years, households have spent about 90 percent of their
disposable income on goods and services, a slightly higher proportion than was spent a hundred years ago. There is little
reason to believe that rising real income will manage to sati-
ate individual wants at any time in the foreseeable future. If
output per manhour were to continue to grow at the four percent
annual rate of the past decade, and if none of this increased
productivity were used to purchase voluntary leisure, median
family income in 1990, expressed in dollars of 1970 purchasing
power, would be $22,000. Such an income is considered handsome
by today's standards, yet few families earning it appear sur-
feited with material possessions. Unfortunately, the society
in which wants are satiated and additional output is of minimal
value is far beyond our current reach. We can only speculate
about longer run prospects. Median family incomes will reach
$50,000, in dollars of 1970 purchasing power, in about 55 years
at present rates of growth. In such a rich society, it is con-
ceivable, though far from certain, that the desire for more material goods will be satiated.

JOB LOCATION

Technical change affects the location of jobs as well as their aggregate number. It is continuously creating jobs in some places and destroying them in others. These dislocations are traceable to the uneven incidence of technical change, and to varying price and income elasticities of demand. The process of job relocation merits a full discussion. First of all, the rate of technical advance is highly uneven. Industries that invest most heavily in research and development experience above average advances in technology, as measured by growth in output per manhour of productivity. Work by George Stigler, John Kendrick, and others at the National Bureau of Economic Research shows that the pressure of competition translates differential rates of productivity increase into differential rates of cost and price reduction.[4] As a result, technically progressive industries have experienced above average expansion in output. If the technical advance is labor saving, less labor is needed per each unit of output, but more units of output are produced. The employment outlook in the technically progressive industries depends on the relative size of the output expansion and labor saving effects. Instances can be cited when the output expansion effect dominated in a spectacular fashion. Equally spectacular dominance by the labor saving effect can also be cited.

Employment will increase if demand is sufficiently responsive to price reductions. Lowering relative price has led to enough expansion of demand to increase employment in such technically progressive industries as airlines, office machinery, and electronic and communications equipment. Historically, the development of new labor saving techniques in manufacturing have often permitted the tapping of previously unexplored segments of the demand schedule, and the transference of work from the home, the farm, the shop, and the office to the factory. Examples include commercial food processing, prefabricated housing components, home permanent kits, and automatic pinsetters in bowling alleys. On the other hand, if demand is not sufficiently elastic, as is often the case in mature industries, productivity increases and price decline will result in less than proportional output gains. Employment will decline. Coal and agriculture are striking examples of industries in

---

[4]George Stigler, *Capital and Rates of Return in Manufacturing Industries*, National Bureau of Economic Research (Princeton, New Jersey: Princeton University Press, 1963); and John W. Kendrick, *Productivity Trends in the United States*, National Bureau of Economic Research (Princeton, New Jersey: Princeton University Press, 1963).

which rapid productivity growth in conjunction with a low price elasticity of demand led to major employment reductions.

There is no general empirical rule stating that rapid productivity increases in an industry lead either to employment increases or decreases in that industry. The relationship between technical change and the location of employment is too rich and varied. Employment in any specific industry is affected by its own technical change but also by progress elsewhere. Reductions in price or improvements in quality have a positive effect on employment when they occur in industries producing inputs or complementary goods, and a negative effect when they occur in industries producing substitutes. Advances in airplane technology increased aluminum production and employment in resort areas while seriously curtailing railroad employment. Consumers sometimes respond to localized increase in productivity by drastically rearranging their purchasing patterns. The result is equally sharp changes in the location of job opportunities. The relative decline in automobile prices during the first half of this century led to widespread automobile ownership. This permitted the substitution of the suburban shopping center for the corner grocery and the downtown department store, greatly altering employment patterns in wholesale and retail trade.

Adjustments to Job Relocation

The continuing relocation of jobs as a result of technical change is not always disruptive. Employment can be reduced in an activity without any resulting frictional unemployment or individual hardship if reductions occur through natural attrition. Jobs opening elsewhere can then be filled by voluntary quits and by the large number of labor market entrants. Employers rely on attrition so long as required employment reductions are relatively modest. Consistent adherance to an attrition policy favorably affects the morale and productivity of current employees and thus future recruiting expenses. Employment is most likely to be reduced by attrition when reductions result from the firm's adoption of new techniques. Employment retrenchment can then precede operation of the new facilities.

Designing and planning the introduction of highly mechanized processes is time-consuming. The gestation period between the initiation of the investment decision and the actual operation of the new facility is frequently as long as one to three years. This time span allows the employer considerable flexibility for planning and for cutting employment by halting the hiring of permanent employees. Interim labor needs can be met by resorting to overtime or by using provisional employees. An attrition policy frequently requires retraining and reassignment, particularly when the new technology requires different skills from the old. However, when the job does not require a different educational background, retraining time is generally minimal and less expensive than firing old workers and hiring new ones. Reliance on attrition is stated company policy in many large firms like General Electric and American Telephone and Telegraph.[5] Also, a small number of studies by the Bureau of Labor Statistics on the installation of automatic technology in a bakery, petroleum refinery, insurance company, electronics plant, and in general company offices disclosed considerable advance planning aimed at avoiding layoffs, and surprisingly few layoffs.[6]

On the other hand, if labor requirements are declining at too rapid a rate in the innovating industry or in its competitors, layoffs result since reliance on attrition becomes economically disadvantageous. Layoffs will also occur when technical advance sharply alters required skills. In particular, if the new job requires considerably more educational background, firms will generally prefer to dismiss current employees and hire new, better educated ones. Workers displaced from one job will have to hunt for another. The faster the rate of technical change, the higher the expected level of frictional unemployment. We conclude that technical change sometimes imposes adjustment burdens on the work force, but not always.

Technical change creates a need for a continuing reconciliation between the composition of labor supply and labor demand. Reconciliation is possible because production can be organized using widely different factor proportions and because the education acquired by most young Americans enables them to learn to perform any of a wide variety of jobs. (Countries with lesser educational achievement are more prone to labor bottlenecks.) The labor market functions flexibly because employers and workers are versatile and are prompted by self-advantage to adjust. Faced with shortages of skilled labor at going wages, employers will increase overtime, or raise wages to attract employees from elsewhere. They may hire less qualified workers, either increasing training expenditures or allowing product quality to decline. Jobs may be redesigned and simplified to make use of available skills.

---

[5] See the statements of Ralph J. Cordiner and C. W. Phalen in *Automation and Society*, eds., Howard B. Jacobson and Joseph S. Roucek (New York: Philosophic Library, 1959).

[6] U.S. Department of Labor, Bureau of Labor Statistics, *Adjustment to the Introduction of Office Automation*, Bulletin No. 1276; and *Impact of Automation*, Bulletin No. 1287 (Washington, D.C.: U.S. Government Printing Office, 1960).

The hospital industry provides a classic example of the
dilution of job content in response to rising wage differentials and the protracted persistence of vacancies. Rising work
loads for resident physicians resulted in more responsibilities
being assigned to interns. Some of the functions previously
performed by interns were then transferred to professional
nurses, intensifying an already rising demand for nurses. As a
result, many of the traditional tasks of the professional nurse
are now being performed by practical nurses or nurses' aides;
the professional nurse functions much as a foreman.[7] These adjustments result in higher unit labor costs, but are undertaken
because they are less expensive than the alternative of lost
production. Likewise, employees who have lost jobs may find it
necessary to change occupation or industry, geographic location,
to undergo training, or to work for lower wages.

In some instances, the reconciliation may not proceed
smoothly. Rapid technical change may lead to structural rather
than frictional unemployment. Displaced workers may be too old,
they may have obsolete skills or be inflexible in their acceptance wage or geographic location. In Chapter 6, we discussed
the fear that the transformation from goods to service production, from blue to white collar work, and from less to more
highly skilled activities might strand the less educated and
the genetically less well-endowed members of the labor force.
The events of the 1960s gave little credence to fears of growing obsolescence and unemployability. Blue collar workers, low
skilled workers, and those with limited educational backgrounds
experienced high unemployment in the 1958-63 period. However,
this pattern was typical for a demand deficiency period, and
the 1964-69 boom restored unemployment among the disadvantaged
and the cyclically sensitive to frictional levels.

THE FUTURE

What of the future? Technical change sharply raising the
marginal product of highly educated workers and lowering that
of the less educated could lead to serious structural unemployment problems. But it is unlikely. A vast expansion in educational attainment is currently underway. Rapid technical
change will be required merely to maintain a high rate of return on education and to provide highly educated workers with
challenging jobs. Indeed, skill requirements may not rise
sharply enough. The pervasiveness and sharpness of the past

---

[7]Donald Yett, "An Economic Analysis of the Hospital Nursing
Shortage" (Ph.D. dissertation: University of California at
Berkeley, 1968).

rise should not be exaggerated. Richard S. Eckaus estimated
that changes in the occupational composition of the work force
between 1940 and 1950 required only a four percent rise in educational attainment.[8] Further, some of the increase in demand
for highly educated workers during the past several decades was
due not to technical change per se but to a special configuration of demand. The defense program, the vast increase in
school enrollment, and the explosion of the research and development and health industries greatly augmented the need for
highly trained workers.

Even so, professional, technical, managerial, and skilled
workers account for only 40 percent of all jobs, and demand is
clearly weakening in some of these education intensive activities. The number of jobs requiring mainly brute strength has
been substantially eroded. In 1900, 8.8 million persons or
30 percent of the work force were farm or nonfarm laborers. By
1970, only 5.1 million persons or seven percent of the work
force were left in these activities. This is past history,
though, and not susceptible to repetition. Sales, service, and
clerical activities have been expanding rapidly, and now account for 36 percent of all employment. Sales, service, and
clerical jobs require more sophisticated skills than do farm or
nonfarm manual labor, but the skills are hardly arcane or
scarce. There is a large number of jobs that call for only a
sense of responsibility, some capacity for dealing with people,
and a modest amount of education. Within the factory itself,
case studies of transition to a new technology do not suggest
any revolutionary rise in skill requirements; they indicate
that there are many innovations and many degrees of automatic-
ity, all differing in their effect on skill requirements.
These studies are consonant with a rise in average skill requirements, although the rise is modest and not pervasive.[9]

Surely this kind of change rather than dramatic upgrading
is what should be expected. Understanding a new process and
the knowledge a worker needs are often inversely related. The
initial operation of new processes requires highly trained and
gifted people capable of making decisions in an environment of
uncertainty and imperfect knowledge. The gradual growth of
understanding particular processes and the experience of early
users eventually leads to the specialization of function and

---

[8]"Economic Criteria for Education and Training," *Review of Economics and Statistics*, May 1964.

[9]See, for example, Howard B. Jacobson and Joseph S. Roucek,
eds., *Automation and Society* (New York: Philosophic Library,
1959); and James R. Bright, *Automation and Management* (Boston:
Harvard Business School, Division of Research, 1958).

the division of labor. The knowledge accumulated results in
routinized and mechanized processes, easily operated. Initially, a high proportion of computer programmers were Ph.D. mathe-
maticians. Today, high school graduates are hired as programmers. When transistors were first being produced commercially,
chemical engineers were necessary to oversee the vats in which
crystals were grown. As processes were sufficiently perfected,
vat supervisors could be given a cookbook of instructions, and
the engineers were replaced with less educated workers. Technical change has two offsetting effects on skill requirements:
the development of new processes raises skill requirements; the
perfection of old processes lowers them.

It is possible that skill raising innovations could predominate to such an extent that skill requirements began to out-
run the capabilities of the work force. If so, relative shortages of highly skilled labor and surpluses of less skilled labor would provide powerful economic incentives for technical
change that would lower skill requirements. As James Bright
reports:

> Machinery manufacturers cannot sell equipment on
> any large scale if extraordinary skills are required
> to operate or maintain it. . . . thus, there is con-
> tinued effort by the machinery designer to simplify
> the operation and maintenance requirements of compli-
> cated machinery, and there is an unpredictable but
> steady downgrading of operator skill requirements
> through machinery improvement in many instances.[10]

It is quite likely that workers who have less than a high
school education will have little difficulty finding employment
in the foreseeable future. Having less than average educational attainment, they will earn less than average incomes and
experience above average unemployment whenever demand is deficient. This is the fate of the back echelon of the hiring
queue. This problem is independent of the rate or type of
technical change, and also of the average level of educational
attainment. Despite the advent of automation, manpower problems may prove to be more tractable in the future than they
were in the past. Our major structural adjustment problems are
fading into history. Workers making the transition from a rural to an urban and industrial economy are probably the group
most prone to structural unemployment or to long spells of frictional unemployment. The Negro laborer and the white subsistence farmer, ejected from farming by the revolution in agricul-
tural technology or attracted by higher urban incomes, bring
with them a heritage of low educational attainment and a lack

---

[10]*Automation and Management*, p. 189.

of exposure to industrial discipline. Their high job turnover
and susceptibility to continuous bouts of unemployment may be
due more to lack of flexibility and work orientation than to
specific skill deficiency. Taking a long view, the transition
to an urban economy is approaching its completion. Structural
adjustment problems may diminish as the country becomes more
geographically integrated, and as a higher proportion of its
workers receive the benefit of urban educational systems and
feel the influence of urban work values.

CONCLUSIONS

For generations, there was a failure to recognize that employment and income insecurity were inherent in post Industrial
Revolution capitalist societies. Unemployment and poverty due
to technical change or other aggregative economic causes were
attributed to individual shiftlessness. Finally, the massive
joblessness of the Great Depression made the defects of the
system perceptible. For the last 40 years, public policy has
been geared increasingly toward restoring the income and employment security that existed prior to the Industrial Revolution. The government has devoted itself to maintaining an adequate number of jobs, guaranteeing some income flow to those
without work, providing appropriate educational backgrounds to
workers, and helping to facilitate the match between job hunters and jobs. The political consensus on the use of monetary
and fiscal policy now ensures that demand deficiency unemployment will be held to socially accepted magnitudes and time intervals. Social security and unemployment compensation provide
some protection against the exigencies of old age and unemployment. The widespread increase in educational level reduces the
risks of capital loss from skill obsolescence. Manpower retraining provides a second chance for those whose skills have
become obsolete.

Public policy is directed toward providing income security
and the opportunity for a job, but does not protect a worker's
right to a specific job. Personnel policies of large corporations and government agencies and collective bargaining agreements are increasingly geared to establishing property claims
to specific jobs for specific workers. The determination of
layoffs on the basis of seniority has created protected en-
claves for employed workers who have lengthy job tenure. Today
over 40 percent of workers covered by major collective bargaining agreements are eligible for the benefits of severance pay
programs, which are generally graduated according to the worker's length of service. Although current benefit payments are
often inadequate, the growth of severance pay programs seems a
more efficient and equitable way of sharing the burden of adjustment to technical change.

The evolution of social and private policies has gone a long way toward making individual economic security consistent with rapid technical progress. Technical change is a disruptive influence on the labor market, but there is no evidence that it is becoming increasingly disruptive. We have experienced two centuries of rapid growth in productivity without signs of increased urban unemployment. Inequities remain, however. The structure of the labor market could certainly be improved. The educational system could be better sensitized to economically relevant training. Nonetheless, we do have an impressive arsenal of policy tools for coping with the disruptive effects of technical change on the labor market. For years, a cultural lag obscured the destabilizing influence of technical change. And now, the same type of lagged perception may prevent us from appreciating how far the social revolution of the past 40 years has gone toward offsetting and minimizing these destabilizing influences.

Index

Katz, Arnold, 60-61
Killingsworth, Charles C.,
  130-131
Kreps, Juanita M., and Joseph H.
  Spengler, 25

Labor, 6 *passim*
  raw, defined, 31
  see also Employment; Hiring;
    Job
Labor demand schedules, 55-56,
  63-65, 87-88, 93
Labor Department, unemployment
  statistics, 99-101
Labor force, 13-19 *passim*
  defined, 15-16
  and labor supply, 15-16
  occupational composition of,
    114-115
  older men in, 25
  subgroups, frictional unem-
    ployment in, 104-106 *passim*
  unemployed, percentages,
    99-101
  women in, 12-13, 16-17, 19,
    26, 28
  see also Employment; Unem-
    ployment; Worker
Labor force participation rate,
  15, 18-19, 25-29
Labor market:
  and commodity market, 90
  data on, collecting, 14-15
  disequilibrium in, 48-49,
    76, 90
  and employer, 55, 63-76
  flexibility of, 135
  full employment in, 78-79
  function of, 53
  inflows and outflows, 49-51
  stocks, 49 *passim*
  teenage, 106-108
  theoretical, 82
Labor market policy, 85, 113,
  116-117, 127
Labor Statistics, Bureau of,
  83, 107, 135
Labor supply:
  defined, 7-8, 15

difficulties in investigating,
  29
elasticity of, 67-69
excess, and structural unemployment, 97-98
and higher wages, 22-23
and labor force, 15-19
and public policy, 19-22
Labor supply schedule:
  backward bending, 22-29
  defined, 7
  in demand deficiency unemploy-
    ment, 87-88
  and hiring ability of firm,
    65-66, 71
  slope of, factors affecting,
    10-11, 67-69, 93
Leisure, 8-10, 24-25
Lipsey, Richard G., 101 n

Manpower Development and Train-
  ing Act (MDTA), 116-117
Mincer, Jacob, 18-19
Minority, *see* Negro, Women
Monetary policy, *see* Policy,
  monetary and fiscal
Monopsonists, 66-68

National Bureau of Economic
  Research, 3, 133
Negroes, 36, 104-106, 108-111,
  116, 138-139
Neighborhood Youth Corps, 117
Nonmarket work, 11-12, 29

Obsolescence, 43-44, *see also*
  Technical change
Output, potential, 24, 88,
  93-94, 131-132

Part-time jobs, 106-108
Policy, labor market, 85, 113,
  116-117, 127
Policy, monetary and fiscal:
  and demand deficiency unem-
    ployment, 95-96, 130
  for income and employment
    security, 139-140
  and inflation, 117-118,
    126-127